Navigating the Patent System

Learn the WHYs of the fundamentals and strategies to protect your invention

James Yang
Patent Attorney

Navigating the Patent System

*Learn the WHYS of the fundamentals
and strategies to protect your invention*
James Yang

Copyright © 2017 James Yang

Visit my website at https://ocpatentlawyer.com

Library of Congress Control Number: 2017915845

ISBN-13: 978-0-9994601-0-8

Printed in the United States of America

Book Design by KarrieRoss.com

First Edition:
10 9 8 7 6 5 4 3 2 1

Disclaimer

This book provides my personal opinions and not the views or opinions of my employer or clients. The opinions in this book cannot therefore be attributed to them. Moreover, my opinions may change over time based on upon further reflection.

This book provides legal information, not legal advice. Attorneys give legal advice only after listening to facts specific to a case, investigating and confirming those facts, reflecting on them, and conducting legal research if necessary. After this process, attorneys give a legal opinion or recommendation. I do not provide any recommended course of action for your situation in this book. For legal advice about your case, you should consult an attorney.

By reading this book, you agree that I am not your attorney and that no attorney-client relationship is formed except by a subsequent written retainer agreement. You agree to not send confidential information unless directed to do so. Communicating with me in any way does not indicate you have retained me as your attorney. If you would like me to represent you, that representation starts *only after execution of a retainer agreement signed by both of us and payment of the requested fee.*

Dedicated to Olga, Daniel, Abigail, and Emily

Contact James Yang

For questions and the latest updates on
Navigating the Patent System,
contact James Yang by visiting:

https://ocpatentlawyer.com

Table of Contents

What is a novelty search?
What is the value of a novelty search?
Informal versus formal novelty searches
Conducting a formal novelty search
Limitations of a formal novelty search
A novelty search is not a clearance search
When to forgo a novelty search
Filing a patent application to protect a revenue stream, even if you
forgo the novelty search

Chapter 4
Trade secrets
Trademarks
Copyrights
Patents
Strategy for utility patent protection
Strategy for design patent protection

Chapter 5
One-year personal grace period
The Three Bars to Patentability: Public use, printed publication, and
offer for sale
Public Use
Printed Publication
Offer for Sale
First-inventor-to-file regime

Chapter 6
Relative novelty versus absolute novelty
Patent cooperation treaty (PCT) application
Costs and consequences of pursing foreign patent protection

Chapter 7
Step 1:The novelty search
Step 2:Prepare and file a patent application
Step 3:Waiting for a first office action from the USPTO and prioritized
examination requests
Step 4:Office action by the USPTO and response by the inventor
Step 5:Application matures to a patent, expires, or is abandoned
Information disclosure statement

Deciding what application to file: Design or utility?

Writing Tip #3:Using the word "may" versus "is"
Writing Tip #4:Preferred embodiments and using the word
"substantial"
Writing Tip #5:Do not use the word, "invention"
Writing Tip #6:Suboptimal embodiments
Writing Tip #7:Ranges
Writing Tip #8:Software Inventions

FAQ #1:How long will it take to get a patent? Is there any way to
speed up the process?
Normal wait time: One to three years or longer
Speeding up the process: Prioritized examination, or, Track One
request
Speeding up the process: Petition to make special based on age
FAQ #2:What does the patent application process cost? If I take a
do-it- yourself (DIY) approach to drafting my patent application,
will it save me money?
Invest in a competent attorney upfront and you will save time and
money in the end
FAQ #3:What exactly am I paying for when I hire a patent attorney?
Experience, experience, experience.
FAQ #4:Do I have a duty to search prior art before I file my patent
application?
No, but if you do, you must disclose your results to the USPTO!
FAQ #5:What happens after the patent application is filed with the
USPTO?
A review of formal requirements by the Office of Initial Patent
Examination
FAQ #6:Can my competitors see the content of my patent
application? Is there any way to keep them in the dark about its
contents and its progress in the patent prosecution process?
Yes, and yes (if you don't file for a patent in foreign countries)!
FAQ #7:What is the relationship between a nonpublication request
and preserving the ability to file for patent protection in foreign
countries?
If you file a nonpublication request, you cannot file for patent
protection in foreign countries
FAQ #8:Should I consider filing for foreign patent protection?
Only if you have established business ties in foreign countries or
another good reason to do so
FAQ #9:How much does it cost to secure foreign patent protection?
Not much to preserve your right to do so, but a lot to secure
foreign patents.
FAQ #10:What is a restriction requirement?

Generally, cornerstone technology
FAQ #25:How does the continuation practice help prevent infringement against my invention?
Maintaining patent pendency of the parent patent application
FAQ #26:How much does the continuation practice cost? Does it have any other benefits?
A few thousand dollars per year, per application
One more benefit: Improved communication with the examiner
FAQ #27:If I didn't file for a continuation application before my patent matured, is there any way to reinstate the patent pendency status of the original patent application?
No. But don't lose all hope!
FAQ #28:How can my own patent be used to reject another one of my own applications?
When it is considered prior art
Dealing with a double patenting rejection
FAQ #29:Can I claim features and aspects invented after filing the patent application?
No!
How to avoid a new matter rejection

Introduction

Congratulations! I am both excited and concerned for you as you begin your journey to protect your invention with a patent. I have been practicing patent law since 2004 and during that time, I have dealt with many startups and understand their budgetary and personnel restraints. My goal is to provide you with the information you need to understand how patents can help you protect your revenue against competitors that may encroach into your market space and cost-effectively secure patent protection.

I am excited by the potential for your business to grow and the personal rewards that come with becoming an inventor. There is a plethora of reasons that someone might want to secure a patent for an invention. You may seek the personal satisfaction of being publicly recognized as an inventor. Some inventors work on inventions with family members as a hobby. Like most other inventors, you most likely want to grow your business or launch a product, a patent could help you make more money. Patents create a barrier to entry, meaning that your competitors cannot enter your market space once you secure your patent. If one of your competitors were to do so, you could sue them for damages and an injunction to force them to pull their product off store shelves. Naturally, this would help your business by reducing competition and enabling you to raise prices on your product.

If your goal is not to manufacture, distribute, or sell your product but rather to collect royalties from a company, a patent allows you to license your idea to another company. With a patent, you can approach larger businesses to offer a license for your invention and prevent them from incorporating your invention into their product without compensation. Without a patent, you would have no enforceable rights and a potential licensee could freely incorporate your idea into their product.

As a startup or solo inventor, your resources are likely not as extensive as that of a large company, putting you at a disadvantage. A patent is an equalizer against larger companies. Such companies have extensive marketing and distribution networks that smaller companies and solo inventors do not have, making it more difficult to compete. Without a patent, a large company would be under no obligation to respect your idea. That is, they would be able to copy your idea without any compensation (i.e., royalties or purchase price) to you. With a patent, you can stop large companies from marketing and selling your invention.

These are all good reasons for seeking a patent, and I am happy for you regardless of the reason you may be seeking a patent for your invention. A successful patent, along with positive reception in the marketplace, can bring significant personal and monetary rewards to you and your family. You may also benefit the public by introducing something new to the marketplace and advancing your field to benefit consumers and businesses.

However, I am also concerned about your future. In my extensive experience helping inventors and small businesses protect their intellectual property, I have seen successful inventors as well as others who have lost a significant amount of money on legal, manufacturing, and marketing fees. In addition to money, failed-business owners have lost time away from loved ones. This time and money, unfortunately, cannot be recuperated.

My goal is not to exaggerate the value of your invention, but rather to guide you through the patent process while minimizing any unnecessary loss of time and money. One of my professional philosophies is to educate inventors, just like you, about their options in the patent process and to offer information about the pros and cons of each option. In this book, I will offer my professional opinions, but ultimately, the decision is yours to make in conjunction with your attorney.

If you are a startup owner, solo inventor, or have a basic knowledge of the patent process, this book is for you. It is not written for other patent attorneys or those with extensive knowledge of the patent process. This book contains information regarding overall patent drafting and examination strategies as well as the logic behind them, but it does not provide information on how to interact with the USPTO (e.g., how to draft a response to an Office Action). Although this book does provide information on the structure of a patent application, the information is presented as a high-level overview and is not intended to be a detailed set of instructions on how to write a patent application.

What you'll find in this book

In the following chapters, you will find explanations of patent laws and rules for the patent process. They are synthesized to demonstrate their ramifications and to offer ways to utilize them to your benefit. The book is divided into three general categories.

Section 1 contains a collection of topics that I call the *Seven Core Concepts*. These Seven Core Concepts encompass foundational patent information necessary for every inventor who goes through the patent process. Additionally, they include the pros and cons of a variety of potential steps before and after you file your patent application. I use the Seven Core Concepts to explain basic patent information, spot common problems, investigate the vision and values of the client, and develop a next-steps plan that is suitable for the inventor.

Section 2 describes my general approach to structuring the content of a patent application. I outline guidelines only, not strict rules. These guidelines explain why some patent application drafting techniques appear counterintuitive but will nonetheless help you review your patent application and communicate your ideas to your patent attorney.

Section 3 is divided into sub-sections that address frequently asked questions (FAQs) about the patent process that I have received over the course of my career. Included are questions regarding whether to file a patent, the patent application process, various office actions including rejections, and options for extending or using your patent once it has been approved. My responses to these questions include general strategies for, and explanations of, the examination process of a patent application.

The information provided in this book is not exhaustive so please check with your patent attorney before implementing any idea in this book.

How to use this book

I recommend reading the entirety of Section 1 to increase your familiarity with the overall patent process. In Sections 2 and 3, you may wish to skip to the headings that are pertinent to you during your application and examination processes. The overall objective of this book is to help you become an informed consumer of patent legal services and learn some of the important legal terms and general aspects of the patent process. With the guidance in this book, my hope is that the information will help you communicate better with your patent attorney so that you will not waste time or money, but rather make the best decisions regarding your patent.

I cannot emphasize enough that this book is not a replacement for competent patent counsel. You should not devise a strategy for protecting your invention based solely on the information or strategies included in this book. Rather, use this book as a guide to devise possible solutions to problems as they arise, address them with your patent attorney, and heed your attorney's advice. Legal advice requires a patent attorney who will listen to you and apply the law to your situation to come up with recommended next steps customized to your situation. Because the information provided is general, and not a response to a question from an inventor, it is not intended as legal advice.

Once again, congratulations on your decision to secure a patent for your invention.

Section 1

To Patent or Not To Patent: The Seven Core Concepts

Purpose of the patent system

The purpose of the patent system is to encourage innovation by granting inventors a patent for their inventions. A patent is a governmental grant to inventors of a right to exclude others from making, using, offering for sale, or selling or importing to, the United States, their invention. The United States is willing to grant a patent to an inventor so that they can use the patent to protect their potential future revenue stream. Patents protect this revenue for a limited time.

In exchange, after the patent term expires, the invention is dedicated to the public. Inventors must teach the public how to make and use the invention so that after the limited time period for which the patents are enforceable has expired, the public can then take advantage of the innovations taught by the inventor.

In this manner, the patent system is a contract with the government. The benefit of the patent system for the government and the public is that new inventions propel technological advances that the public can use after the expiration of the patent. The benefit to inventors is that they are granted an "exclusionary right" (not unlike a monopoly) over the patented invention for a limited time.[1]

The basis for the United States patent system is Article I, Section 8, Clause 8 of the U.S. Constitution, which grants Congress the power "to promote the progress of science and useful arts, by securing for limited times to authors and inventors the exclusive right to their respective writings and discoveries."

Benefits to the patent owner

The patent enables inventors to level the playing field against larger competitors. Inventors may use their exclusionary rights over an invention to create a "barrier to entry" (i.e., block others from competing in the market with their version of a competing product) against their competitors, increase their revenue, and even threaten large corporations with patent infringement if they infringe on the inventor's patent.

Barrier to entry
The first benefit of an exclusionary right is that it erects a barrier to entry so that others cannot compete against the inventor by introducing the patented product into the marketplace. If competitors do enter the market, the inventor can utilize the patent against competitors and make them "disgorge" (i.e., give back) profits and enjoin them from engaging in (i.e., stop further) sales and marketing efforts.

However, a patent is not immediately granted upon filing a patent application. Rather, the patent right "vests with" (i.e., is conferred upon) the inventor when the patent application matures into a patent, which could take from nine months to five years. In the meantime, while the invention is patent pending, competitors can appropriate the invention without penalty. Once the patent is granted, the inventor can sue the competitor for patent infringement, collect damages, and enjoin the competitor from continuing to market the patented invention.

Although the inventor cannot sue the competitor immediately after filing the patent application, this is not a good reason to forgo patenting the invention. Filing a patent may be an important part of a successful business plan, despite the length of time it takes for a patent application to mature into a patent. For example, competitors marketing the invention before the United States Patent and Trademark Office (USPTO) has granted the patent may later become licensees that must pay royalties on the issued patent. Competitors who market the invention before the patent issues also help create a demand for the patented invention, which may benefit the patent applicant when the patent is granted and these competitors become potential licensees. However, if it is critical that the patent mature as soon as possible, there are ways to shorten the period between the filing of the application and its examination. (This is explained in Chapter 7, which covers the overall patent process.) Be warned that if an inventor begins marketing a product without seeking a patent, he or she will eventually forfeit the ability to secure a patent and the invention will be dedicated to the public. (Please see Chapter 5 for more information regarding such bars to patentability.)

Increased revenue

If there is a large enough demand for a patented invention, the patent itself may increase the gross revenue of the product. If an invention is not patented, competitors may enter the marketplace offering products similar to the invention. When this happens, prices drop because competitors are trying to make their products more attractive to potential consumers. However, if the invention is patented, competitors can be sued for patent infringement and enjoined from selling the product in the marketplace. Therefore, competition is reduced and the inventor may theoretically charge a higher price for the product until the patent expires.

Leveled playing field with large corporations

In the marketplace, large corporations often have many advantages over those of a small company. They have funding, marketing relationships, distribution channels, and expertise beyond those of a small company or solo inventor. If a small company or solo inventor were to market the same product as a large corporation, the small company or solo inventor would likely lose to the large corporation, which would capture more market share of the product.

However, if a large corporation were to introduce a product that infringed on a small company or solo inventor's patent, the patent owner would be able to sue the large corporation for patent infringement. Although the cost for patent litigation is high, there are contingency fee patent litigators that can reduce the financial burden of this litigation.

With these benefits in mind, I will enumerate and explain the Seven Core Concepts, which, in conjunction with the counsel of a patent attorney, will help inventors decide how to best protect their invention.

Overview of The Seven Core Concepts

The Seven Core Concepts are a collection of topics containing essential information that all inventors seeking to protect their ideas, inventions, and other intellectual property should know. With an understanding of the Seven Core Concepts, inventors can make informed decisions regarding whether to file a patent application, launch a new business, start a new product line, or how much time and money to invest in their invention.

I developed The Seven Core Concepts during my extensive experience conducting over 700 consultations with solo inventors and small businesses over a period of thirteen years. Each client approaches the patent process in a different way. One person may consider the patent process a necessary evil. Some may believe that the entire patent process is a waste of time and money, while others may understand the value of a patent. Another person may approach the patent process without any preconceived notions at all. Regardless of how one approaches the patent process, most clients have similar questions and concerns. I attempt to answer those questions with the Seven Core Concepts. They include important patent information and are educational tools for clients to make smart legal decisions. They may also help clients identify common pitfalls they should be aware of during the patent process. Although most clients ask similar questions to which there are technically correct legal answers, I attempt to discern and address the true concerns and goals behind their questions when offering responses. This is because the recommended course of action for any client depends on that client's vision and values. I therefore include different possible courses of action tailored to businesses with different goals.

Early in my patent career, I had a cookie-cutter approach to client counseling. My recommendations were the same for each client: conduct a novelty search and file a patent application. This advice did not always yield the best results. My previous, standard recommendations did not take into consideration clients' distinct visions and values. When I began taking these into account, I altered my recommendations and produced better results and therefore much happier clients.

Eventually, as I began to better interact with clients and understand their needs, I developed a more holistic approach by which I could uncover a client's perspective and business goals. The legal services and costs associated with the patent process began to better fit their needs. To uncover a client's visions and values, the Seven Core Concepts were used to examine the client's financial and marketing constraints and to decide what the client might do when faced with various scenarios. During the initial consultations, clients and I jointly develop a plan of next steps to help clients achieve their goals. Using the Seven Core Concepts, I consult with clients so that, together, we can formulate collaborative, individual plans and so that clients understand each step and why it is desirable to expend funds at each stage of the process. The Seven Core Concepts are as follows:

Core Concept 1: Defining the invention

The purpose of this concept is identification of the point of novelty of the invention. Pinpointing its novelty specifies how the invention is an improvement over existing technology. Clients often come to my office with prototypes of their inventions. My job is to sift through all the information they provide and help inventors define the point(s) of novelty of their inventions. This could be one or more aspects of an invention, but the invention's point of novelty is always related to its crux or essence—that is, the part of the invention that (1) makes the invention work and (2) distinguishes it from other existing technology. In Chapter 1, I will go into greater detail about the point of novelty and how to identify it.

Core Concept 2: Resolving ownership issues

To file a patent application, the client must own the rights to the idea or invention. In most cases, this is not a problem. However, in certain situations, ownership of the invention may be "fractured," or divided between several people. For example, an independent contractor, co- inventor, or employee may own some rights to the invention despite not thinking of the initial idea and perhaps only contributing improvements for parts of the idea or invention. (That is, unless there has been an agreement to assign the invention to the hiring company or individual. See Chapter 2.) In Chapter 2, I will show how to identify common issues related to ownership as well as offer possible solutions.

Core Concept 3: Conducting a novelty search

A novelty search is a search for published documents (e.g., issued patents and pre-grant publications) to determine if the invention is novel and, in certain cases, if it is a significant advancement (i.e., non-obvious) given existing technology. In Chapter 3, I will cover the following questions: When is a novelty search necessary? What are its benefits? How reliable is a novelty search for predicting whether the invention is novel or non-obvious?

Core Concept 4: Exploring different ways to protect your idea

There are four main areas of Intellectual Property (IP) law useful for protecting ideas and inventions. These include: trade secrets, trademarks, copyrights, and patents. Each type protects ideas or inventions in different ways and provides a different remedy for infringement. The recommended course of action for protecting an idea or invention may include pursuing one or more of the four types of IP rights. In Chapter 4, I will explain each type of IP protection and cover the basics of each. However, I will focus primarily on protecting an idea with design and utility patents.

Core Concept 5: Bars to patentability and the impact of the first-inventor-to-file regime

In 2013, the United States transitioned from a first-to-invent (FTI) regime to a first-inventor-to-file (FITF) regime. This transition changed how startups and solo inventors needed to think about protecting their ideas and inventions with patents. In Chapter 5, I will go into detail about this significant change, explain its effects on the patent process, and describe the order in which marketing and filing a patent application should occur.

Core Concept 6: Preserving foreign patent protection

Seeking foreign patent protection can be expensive. Its value varies and depends on the strength of existing business relationships as well as the goals of the inventor. However, as I outline in Chapter 6, preserving your ability to seek foreign protection does not necessarily require a significant expenditure, and is often recommended.

Core Concept 7: Reviewing the overall patent process

The entire patent process can be very long and costly. In Chapter 7, I cover the major steps of the preparation of a patent application and the examination phase at the USPTO. I also outline the timing of major events involving the USPTO as well as expected costs of preparing, examining, and maintaining a patent.

CHAPTER 1

Core Concept 1:
Defining the Invention

A common problem in trying to broadly protect one's invention is the lack of focus on the point of novelty of the invention. Without a clear description of what the invention is in its most basic elements, the patent application will not have a clear focus, the claims will not be broad, and prosecution may stray from the most important aspects of the invention.

Inventions are usually designed for a primary use (i.e., initial field of use or vertical market) but may also be used in ways beyond the inventor's original intention. For example, a pencil may initially be designed for use in an academic setting, but upon further exploration, a modified version of the invention may also be used in a construction setting. This expanded utility increases the potential for an inventor to make money from the sale of that invention and may motivate the inventor to think of other bells and whistles for the invention and further broaden its applicability. Many inventors find this possibility exciting and may expend an inordinate amount of time and energy brainstorming ideas. They are often excited to introduce the new product into the marketplace and want to be sure they have thought through the full range of applications of the invention.

However, the excessive exploration of the invention's possible utilities may cause the inventor to lose sight of the primary utility and prevent the inventor from properly identifying the point of novelty. Sometimes, in these cases, the invention takes on a life of its own. Instead of remaining focused on the point of novelty, the inventor may be distracted by the secondary aspects. These secondary aspects may be interesting, but are nonetheless ancillary and are not crucial to the point of novelty of the invention.

Keeping an eye on the point of novelty of the invention is important because, as I discuss below, it helps structure the patent application and dictates the examination and overall strategies for protecting the invention. A part of my job is to keep the inventor focused on the invention's point of novelty. Otherwise, decisions and key points of the patent process may be based on something other than the point of novelty, complicating the patent process and jeopardizing the scope of protection afforded by the patent.

What is the point of novelty?

The point of novelty is the invention's "secret sauce," the principle operation of the invention, and the glue that binds the entire product together. The point of novelty must be the guiding point of reference when developing the patent claims in the patent application, the examination strategy, and the basic structure of the patent application. If the point of novelty is not identified correctly, the structure of the patent application, the "metes and bounds" (i.e., the focus of the claims that define a patent's scope of protection) of what is being claimed as the invention, and the progress of the patent examination process may produce less than stellar results. This, in turn, could cost time and money to fix, if a fix is even possible, especially if the application has already been filed. Deficiencies in the patent application caused by an inaccurate identification of the point of novelty may be irreparable and narrow the claims of the patent so as to be meaningless to the inventor.

Identifying the point of novelty: Focusing on the invention's benefit over prior art

To begin to understand how to identify the point of novelty of the invention, I will walk through the mental steps that I take using an example of a hypothetical mechanical pencil featured on the left side of Figure 1 below.

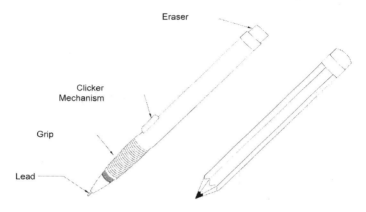

Figure 1

One way to identify the point of novelty is to work backward from a new benefit of an invention not provided by existing products or technology. For example, the problem with writing instruments prior to the invention of mechanical clicker system was the time spent sharpening the pencil. The benefit of a mechanical pencil over a wooden pencil is the elimination of this step for the user. The mechanical pencil always stays sharp because it has a mechanical clicker system (i.e., solution) that extends the proper amount of lead upon each click. In this example, the mechanical clicker system is the point of novelty.

In this hypothetical case, a basic wooden pencil, pictured on the right in Figure 1, is considered the "prior art" for the mechanical pencil invention. Prior art is anything that can be used by the USPTO to reject a patent claim or invalidate an issued patent during litigation. Generally, prior art includes current patent applications and granted patents on existing technology that are available to the public prior to the filing date of the patent application. The point of novelty is the "point of departure" (i.e., that which makes the invention different) from the prior art. The claims presented in the patent application and the patent should focus on (i.e., should be directed to) the point of novelty. Otherwise, the claims presented in the patent application and the patent are not fully protecting the invention.

During the inventing process, inventors may brainstorm other secondary features to include in the application such as a specialized grip for the fingers or an eraser that can be removed and attached to the top end of the pencil. The inventor may get off track and begin to attribute more importance to the grip or removable eraser, for example, than to the mechanical pencil's primary point of novelty (i.e., the mechanical clicker system so that the mechanical pencil is ever-sharp). Does the grip enable the mechanical pencil to remain forever sharp? No. Does the removable eraser enable this benefit? No. Does the mechanical clicker system enable this benefit? Yes. It is important to focus on the primary benefit of the invention (i.e., the mechanical pencil remains forever sharp) and work backwards to the part of the structure (i.e., the mechanical clicker system) that achieves that benefit. If more importance is erroneously attributed to the grip or the removable eraser, the inventor may be tempted to focus the claims of the patent application on these ancillary features instead of the mechanical clicker system. If the focus of the claims of the patent application is shifted away from the point of novelty, any patent that matures based on these shifted claims may provide inadequate patent protection.

The point of novelty is the structuring principle of your patent application

By identifying and focusing on the point of novelty, the structure of the patent application and its claims will more likely provide a focused, meaningful scope of patent protection for the invention because they are directed at protecting the invention's key feature. Any temptation to shift the claim scope to a feature other than the point of novelty should be resisted. The inventor should stay focused on the point of novelty and draft the patent application to draw attention to the point of novelty. Am I saying that the application should not include other features of the invention or pencil? Absolutely not. If these secondary features, such as the grip and removable eraser, as in the example of the mechanical pencil, are beneficial to customers, they should be included in the patent application. However, they should be described in such a way that it is obvious they are secondary in importance to the identified point of novelty.

Furthermore, refinements to the point of novelty should be included and expanded upon in the patent application. For example, there may be a tongue and groove configuration added onto the mechanical clicker system that helps the mechanical clicker system work better. This configuration should be included in the patent application. Furthermore, the patent application should include its reverse: the groove and tongue configuration. Although describing the reverse situation costs more time and money, it would be a worthwhile investment since the reverse situation may be directly related to the point of novelty.

This same principle applies to materials, orientations, and other aspects of the invention that may be directly or indirectly related to the point of novelty. Simply put, once the point of novelty is identified, the patent application should focus primarily on the details of the point of novelty and secondarily on ancillary aspects of the invention. However, for these secondary features not directly related to the point of novelty, the time and expense of including them in the application may not be worth their inclusion.[2]

Finally, the point of novelty is also useful for identifying a minimally viable or sub-optimal product that could still be a viable competitive alternative to the proposed invention. Inventors often believe that their invention is the best in a particular metric (e.g., speed, ease-of-use, etc.). Inventors want to, and should, protect this benefit. However, inventors should also think about protecting sub-optimal versions of their inventions or products. The patent application should therefore include information related to the preferred version of the invention along with other versions that may be less optimal, but would still be able to compete in the marketplace. For example, if an inventor conceives of a way to build the fastest car and wants to patent it, and if a corresponding patent protects only the fastest car, competitors could introduce the second-fastest car at a lower cost. These companies would avoid patent infringement liability and still compete for customers who do not want to spend more money on the fastest car, but are willing to spend substantially less for the second fastest. In other words, customers may choose to buy a product that is slightly inferior for a significantly lower price. To prevent such competition, patents should be broad enough to encompass products that are slightly slower or slightly less easy to use, but that nevertheless incorporate the point of novelty. This is done by disclosing and claiming the point of novelty in the patent application broadly enough to encompass the minimally viable product.

The importance of accurately identifying the right point of novelty when crafting the claims in a patent application

To fully understand the importance of properly identifying the point of novelty, one should understand the balance we, as patent attorneys, try to achieve for clients. On one hand, patent attorneys try to present a narrow claim that does not encompass the prior art (i.e., information that is in the public domain) or is not an obvious variant of the prior art. If this occurred, the claimed invention would be rejected for being either not novel or an obvious variant of the prior art. On the other hand, the claims must be broad enough so that the scope of patent protection afforded under the patent would adequately prevent others from competing with the inventor.

The patent examiner decides whether a claim is so broad that existing technology or information would anticipate (i.e., already includes or discloses) the claimed invention. In other words, the examiner might reject the patent application by alleging that certain prior art references show that the claimed invention is not novel or is an obvious variant of an already existing idea. A simple way to visualize this examination process is to ask whether the claim in the patent application is so broad that existing technology would infringe on it if the claim were to mature into a patent. If so, the maturation of the patent would be unjust because manufacturers of existing products would suddenly be infringing on the claims of the patent. The claims need to be narrow enough so that the issued patent would not encompass preexisting technology.

However, the goal of the patent process is to secure meaningfully broad patent protection over the invention such that competitors would find it difficult to copy or make minor modifications while avoiding patent infringement liability. Simply put, patent attorneys do not want to secure claims that are so narrow that competitors may use the invention without liability by designing around the patent. Rather, our goal is to secure claims that are meaningfully broad (not too broad or too narrow) to make it difficult for competitors to design around the patent claims, yet also ensure that the application has the ability to mature into a patent and not be rejected due to prior art.

In the above example of the mechanical pencil, if the point of novelty is the mechanical clicker system and a decision must be made to narrow the claims, everyone involved needs to make sure that the claims remain focused on the point of novelty. This means including limitations on the claims that are related only to the point of novelty and not secondary features, which would significantly narrow the scope of the claims. For example, suppose the claim is amended to include a secondary feature, such as the grip on the mechanical pencil. If the competitor then incorporates a different form of the grip while using the same mechanical clicker system, this competitor would avoid patent infringement liability.

The patent attorney needs to find the right balance so that the patent claims are not so narrow as to be easy to design around or so broad as to encompass existing technology. If the point of novelty of the invention is improperly identified, this balance may be lost and leave the inventor without meaningful protection.

CHAPTER 2

Core Concept 2:
Ownership—Resolving Ownership Issues

The big problem here is that ownership of the rights to the invention may arise and vest with multiple people because of the way that the invention was created. However, to fully exploit the inventive technology, those that contributed to the invention should assign the invention rights to a single entity, such as a person or a corporation. Otherwise, the co-inventors can destroy the value of the invention and harm the other owner(s).

Ownership is one of the concepts that should be clarified and investigated prior to the filing of a patent application. The reason is that if a single inventor does not entirely own the invention rights he or she cannot effectively seek patent protection for the idea. When there are multiple inventors, inventive rights vest (i.e., belong) to the inventors who conceive of the invention. Invention rights split between multiple inventors (i.e., not controlled by any one entity) arise from relationships such as co-inventorship, investor–inventor relationships, independent contractors, and employer–employee relationships and may cause the inventors from exploiting the technology for fear of what the other co-owners might do to harm the others if there is a disagreement. To avoid these problems, these inventive rights should be transferred to a single entity by "assignment," as explained below.

Co-inventorship

"Co-inventorship" is the situation where two or more people collectively come up with an idea to solve a problem. This group of people is known as the "inventive entity." At the beginning, each inventor included in the inventive entity owns one hundred percent of the invention. Each of the co-inventors may think that he or she does not want to harm the other inventor(s), but over time feelings may change. Business pressures and personal problems may impose new duties and obligations on the co- inventors. Fights and disagreements may cause co-inventors to have very different views on how to commercialize the patent(s) or market products under the patent. Another downside to co-inventorship is that under United States law, each inventor can market and sell the patented invention without accounting for, or sharing, his or her profits with the other inventor(s). Additionally, any of the inventors can act against the interest of any other co-inventor by dedicating the invention to the public (i.e., allowing it to be designated part of the public domain) without permission from a co-inventor.

To mitigate potential disagreements, the co-inventors may enter into a "joint exploitation agreement." In this agreement, the co-inventors mutually agree that they will not dedicate the invention to the public. They also agree that they will not market or sell the invention separately. Another more common means of protecting co-inventors is to form a corporate entity (e.g., L.L.C., S–Corporation, etc.) and assign the invention rights to the corporation. In this case, the co-inventors will split the shares of the corporation and, through the corporate structure, determine the rights and responsibilities of each of the co-inventors. This may deter inventors from harming the patented invention owned by the business due to their duty of loyalty to the corporation.

Inventor-investor relationships

Ownership conflicts may also arise in inventor-investor relationships. An inventor may contribute the invention rights to the business while the investor contributes monetary funds. In other words, the inventor puts forth sweat equity and the rights to the invention, whereas the investor puts forth monetary equity. However, the inventor owns the inventive rights unless he or she assigns them to another person.

To protect both parties, the inventor should not assign any percentage (i.e., less than 100%) of the invention rights to an investor even if the investor is asking for this. Doing so would not be optimal for the inventor or the investor. If there is a disagreement between the investor and inventor, they can each harm the invention's value by dedicating the inventive rights to the public or licensing the rights to a competitor without accounting for profits to the other co-inventor.

An assignment of 100% of the rights to the investor can hurt the inventor, as well. The investor can now sell or license the rights to the invention to a third party without compensation to the inventor or start a new company without the inventor. This is not a good situation for the inventor. In this case, the inventor now has no ownership rights or interest in the patent rights and the investor can harm the inventor.

To avoid these types of situations, the inventor should assign the invention rights to a corporation. At the corporate level, the shares, money, and/or employment opportunities can be divided as desired, and the rights and responsibilities of the all parties decided. Their duty of loyalty to the corporation prevents both parties from doing things that might devalue the invention.

Independent contractors

Ownership issues could also arise in a relationship between an inventor and an independent contractor (e.g., consultant, engineer, designer). As established, the inventive rights vest with the person that conceives of the invention, unless an assignment occurs. An independent contractor who conceives of an invention, even a small part, owns his or her part of the invention. If that part of the invention is incorporated into the inventor's patent application, and the application later matures into a patent, the independent contractor owns the entire patent along with any other inventor. To avoid this, the inventor should request that the independent contractor sign an "invention assignment agreement." In this agreement, the independent contractor "agrees to assign and does hereby assign" the inventive rights to the company when the independent contractor conceives of an invention. This is a common requirement in independent contractor agreements and many independent contractors do not take issue with signing an invention assignment agreement. That is, of course, unless the assignment is so broad that the independent contractor would be precluded from seeking employment from other companies. The agreement should be reasonable in scope and seek only to assign inventive rights (solely applicable to the job they were hired for) to the hiring company.

    If the independent contractor is unwilling to execute an assignment agreement, then a suitable solution may be an agreement that you would have a license to any technology the independent contractor incorporated into your product. The purpose of this fall-back position is to allow you to go to any other independent contractor and not be locked into a particular independent contractor.

Employer-employee relationships

Conflicts may also occur in employer-employee relationships. Many companies at their inception are small and funds are tight. These companies may not have formal employer-employee agreements wherein the employee agrees to assign all invention rights to the company. As companies grow, they may rely on goodwill and tight-knit relationships between employers and the employees. However, this goodwill is not enforceable in a court of law. Employers should therefore enter into an invention assignment agreement with employees. Without it, the employee may retain his or her invention and the invention rights would not belong to the employer. These assignment agreements are desirable for project developers, sales personnel who come up with ways to improve the company's product, and/or employees involved in manufacturing who might have insight into the most efficient way of making products.

CHAPTER 3

Core Concept 3:
Conducting a Novelty Search

Misunderstanding the purpose of a formal novelty search is a common problem. The results of the novelty search determine, at most, the likelihood of patentability, but do not offer a guarantee. At the very least, the inventor should conduct an informal search. Use the seven-step patent search strategy, published by the USPTO, and discussed below, to do a free, informal, do-it-yourself search before seeking the paid advice of a patent attorney.

The first step in the patent process is a novelty search, which is not required to file a patent application, but may be beneficial in certain cases. This chapter provides information that will help inventors decide whether to conduct a formal paid search. I will describe the goals, limitations, and benefits of a novelty search, which may help inventors avoid unrealistic expectations that could waste their time and money.

What is a novelty search?

There are four criteria that must be met to obtain a patent on an invention:

1. The invention must be eligible for patent protection (i.e., it must be patentable subject matter).

2. The invention must be novel.
3. The invention must be non-obvious (i.e., it must be a significant advancement of existing technology).
4. A patent application must be filed with the U.S. Patent and Trademark Office (USPTO). The application must meet certain other formal standards and be examined by the USPTO.

A novelty search will help a potential applicant determine if their invention meets the second requirement mentioned above—that an invention must be novel. The searcher attempts to find patent documents that teach how to make and use your invention (i.e., that disclose the point of novelty). The goal is not to determine whether an invention is non-obvious (criteria number 3 above), though references that are similar to the point of novelty may be uncovered. These similar references could be the basis for an obviousness determination. However, it is too difficult (and sometimes impossible) to render an opinion as to whether the combination of similar prior art documents would indicate that the proposed invention is an obvious variant. The determination of whether multiple, combined prior art documents would render the invention "obvious" is highly subjective and dependent upon the examiner assigned to a patent application.

To reiterate, a novelty search entails looking through the prior art with the primary objective of determining whether an invention is new or novel with respect to existing technology. Prior art includes all existing information including that found in any public domain (i.e., published and not secret) or pertaining to existing technology. This information can be used to reject an application for patent. In our example, the idea of a basic wooden pencil is in the public domain and is prior art to the mechanical pencil.

Prior art also includes secret prior art. For example, when a patent application is initially filed with the USPTO, the patent application is not immediately open to the public. It remains secret for a period of eighteen months after which the patent application is published even if the patent application does not mature into a patent. During that eighteen-month period, the patent application is considered to be secret prior art. Even though secret prior art is not publicly accessible, it can be used to reject a later filed patent application if the first secret patent application later matures and becomes public or published. In other words, when a patent is issued or published, it is retroactively considered prior art as of its filing date. However, someone conducting a novelty search will not be able to find such references because that secret reference would not yet be published at the time the novelty search is conducted. Although it would be desirable to be able to uncover these hidden references, it is nonetheless a risk that one must accept and adjust to during the examination process.

The novelty search typically involves searching the patent document databases at the USPTO and perhaps foreign patent documents. At the USPTO website, the patents and the pre-grant publications are in separate databases. Because some mature into a patent and others do not, and because some patents are issued but are never published, both databases should be searched if inventors attempt to conduct novelty searches themselves. An easier database to use for searching is www.freepatentsonline.com.

The searchable portion of the USPTO databases only includes issued patents and applications published during a limited time span. Issued patents are word-searchable only from the early 1970s onward, while published applications are word-searchable from the early 2000s, when publication of applications began. For those interested in doing their own informal novelty search, the Seven Step Patent Search

Strategy, published on the USPTO.gov website, offers instructions.

As of 2017, there are over nine million issued U.S. patents and many pre-grant publications in the patent document databases at the USPTO. Even though a novelty search does not typically extend beyond the patent document databases at the USPTO, such a search is still relatively reliable because of the large volume of information contained in the nine million patent documents at the USPTO.

What is the value of a novelty search?

There are several reasons to conduct a novelty search. First, the novelty search may reveal documentation of prior art that includes an identical description of the point of novelty of the proposed invention. In this case, the patent search saves the inventor the cost of filing a patent application. Moreover, this revelation may inspire the inventor to modify the current idea or pursue another invention. This would not only save the inventor the costs of preparing and filing the patent application and patent prosecution, but also the time, energy, and money that the inventor would have wasted building and marketing the invention. The inventor can divert this time, energy, and money to building and marketing a different invention.

Because the novelty search provides insight into existing technology (i.e., the state-of-the-art related to the invention), it helps when drafting the patent application. Now, we know what not to focus on. This may help the drafter to focus on those points of novelty of the invention (as discussed in Chapter 1) that may have a greater likelihood of receiving a patent.

Informal versus formal novelty searches

When inventors conduct their own informal novelty search, they typically conduct a generic, text-based search using an online search engine such as Google. However, such a generic search may produce a long list of results that include irrelevant references. For example, if one were to search the term "butterfly," the results may include references related to both a butterfly valve in a fluidic system (as in a car, for example) and the insect called a butterfly. It would be an inefficient use of time to sift through all the results to find all the relevant references. Of course, an inventor should always conduct a short, cursory, informal search before paying for a formal one. If something is found that would prevent the inventor from securing a patent, then he or she may avoid wasting money on attorney fees to conduct a *formal* novelty search.

Yet if nothing relevant is uncovered in an informal search, the next step may be a formal search conducted by a patent attorney. This is because the proper way to conduct a novelty search is by way of a more comprehensive class/subclass search.[3] A class delineates one technology from another. A subclass delineates processes, structural features, and functional features of the subject matter encompassed within the scope of the class. A formal novelty search identifies the proper class and subclass combinations for the invention, which then produces more concise search results. A text-based search conducted according to the proper classes and subclasses produces highly relevant search results compared to an informal novelty search.

For this reason, a formal novelty search provides more reliable information so that inventors can make informed decisions whether to file a patent application and spend time and money launching a product. Does this mean that a formal novelty search is reliable enough to guarantee a patent on the invention? No, a formal novelty search does not guarantee that a patent will be granted for the invention, even if it yields no relevant references that disclose the proposed invention's point of novelty. A formal novelty search is not able to uncover every relevant prior art reference for any given invention. There are about 450 different classes and one thousand subclasses of patent documents categories. Some of the proper class/subclass combinations of the invention may be inadvertently overlooked and not searched. Or, some searchable, relevant references may be incorrectly classified. Additionally, even if all the proper class/subclass combinations of the invention have been identified and searched, particular search terms may not yield all relevant prior art documents if different descriptive terms and phrases were used.

Therefore, a formal novelty search that uncovers no prior art references is not a guarantee that a patent will be granted for the invention. If the novelty search does not uncover any reference that discloses the point of novelty, and an attorney offers an opinion that the invention is novel based on that search, that opinion indicates only a likelihood that a patent *may* be granted should an application for patent be filed and other patent requirements satisfied. Anecdotally, if the search results in a positive opinion of patentability, I would say there is roughly a seventy percent likelihood that the patent will be granted. Conversely, there is roughly a thirty percent chance that the USPTO will find a more relevant reference not uncovered by the formal novelty search and therefore not grant a patent. Inventors should understand that a formal novelty search that uncovers no relevant references to prior art offers only a likely outcome of a granted patent. That is, it is more *likely* than not that a patent will mature should an application for patent be filed with the USPTO.

Conducting a formal novelty search

To conduct a proper novelty search, one should appropriately identify the point of novelty of the invention, as discussed in Chapter 1. If something other than the point of novelty is searched, the novelty search process will more than likely produce suboptimal results because it would uncover prior art documents not related to the point of novelty, which would not be significantly useful in rendering an opinion regarding patentability of the invention.

Once the point of novelty is identified, the novelty search is typically a two-step process. The first step is searching patent databases at the USPTO and sometimes foreign patent databases for prior art documents that are similar to the point of novelty of the invention. This step is not normally conducted by a patent attorney but is usually outsourced to a third-party, prior art, search company that bills at a lower rate than an attorney's office. In addition, these third-party prior art search companies have software that can review a larger number of patent documents more efficiently.[4] The second step is the review stage in which a patent attorney reviews the search results from the patent search company. The attorney will determine whether any of the prior art references include patent documents that disclose the point of novelty of the proposed invention. If so, it is unlikely that the USPTO would grant a patent on the invention.

Limitations of a formal novelty search

Even if a formal novelty search is conducted and no prior art references are found (indicating the likelihood that a patent would be granted on the invention), the initial opinion (i.e., office action) of the examiner at the USPTO may still be that the invention is not novel or is obvious in light of the prior art. This could happen because the initial claims in the patent application are designed to come close to, but not clearly avoid, the point of novelty of the prior art. The patent attorney may strategically draft the claim rather broadly so that an initial rejection of the claims is expected. The claims can always be narrowed afterward to avoid the prior art during examination to secure the patent.

Let me explain: a strategy when representing solo inventors and small companies is to secure claims of medium breadth—not too narrow or too broad. On one hand, claims that are narrow are more likely to be granted a patent by the USPTO. However, narrow patent claims are easy for competitor's design around and so avoid patent infringement liability. If narrow claims are sought, this does not provide significant barriers to competitors introducing similar products into the market place. On the other hand, *broad* patent claims are great for solo inventors and small companies since they are difficult to design around. Broad patent claims create obstacles for others to compete with the inventor (i.e., an effective barrier to entry from competitors). However, very broad patents are expensive because they require extensive argumentation, including back- and-forth communications with the USPTO. This increases the time that an attorney spends on the case and the costs for the inventor. When drafting the initial patent application, I attempt to find a good balance between these broad and narrow claims to provide a cost-effective strategy to secure a meaningful barrier to entry from competitors.

This strategy seeks allowance of a claim that is as close to the prior art as possible. If the examiner rejects the claim because it is too broad and encompasses the prior art, the claims can be narrowed during examination to avoid the prior art and to convince the examiner to issue the patent. This strategy allows the attorney to narrow the claims only to the extent that it conflicts with the prior art cited by the examiner and negotiate the broadest possible claim coverage. This, at least, is the goal. For this reason, the initial claims are designed so that they are likely to be rejected by the examiner. The novelty search is therefore not indicative of whether the initial office action from the USPTO will be a rejection or an allowance. A positive opinion from a novelty search primarily indicates the likelihood that the patent application may *eventually* mature into a patent, not the likelihood that the original claims submitted with the patent application will be allowed as patentable in the initial office action.

A novelty search is not a clearance search

Inventors may feel that it is appropriate to address concerns about infringing on another unknown patent with their attorney when the topic of a novelty search arises. However, novelty and clearance searches should not be confused with each other because they are not directly related.

While a formal novelty search reveals the likelihood that the claims of a patent application may be *allowed* by the USPTO to mature into a patent, a "clearance search" helps determine the likelihood that if an invention is made, used, sold, or offered for sale in, or imported into, the United States, such actions would *infringe* on patent claims owned by others. Allowability and infringement are completely different issues and should not be conflated.

A patent may be granted on an invention that infringes on another patent. The patent may be granted for the invention because it improves on an existing patented product or adds a feature to that prior product. Clearance searches are significantly more expensive than prior art searches because they require more onerous tasks: sifting through many patent references, checking patent terms to see if patents of interest are still in force, checking the scope of the patent claims, comparing the patent claims to the invention, and, if needed, reviewing the prosecution history to construe the claims to determine if the claims encompass your product. Clearance searches are cost-prohibitive for most clients and are therefore normally not often conducted.

However, a scaled-down approach to addressing potential infringement may be cost-effective. If the inventor or company knows of a similar product or competitor that has a patent pending or a patent, it may be worthwhile to conduct an "assignee search" (i.e., to look for the patent documents assigned to specific competitors). The assignee search is a search of the patent databases for any patents or patent application filings owned by a competitor. Additionally, the patent pending product and its packaging may be searched for any patent markings. Once relevant patent documents are found, the claims of that patent(s) or pending application may be analyzed for actual or potential infringement concerns.

Side Note: A novelty search may loosely be used as a clearance search. Although I have indicated that questions related to patentability should not be discussed in relation to questions related to infringement, if an inventor believes that the point of novelty of his or her invention is worth seeking a patent, the applicants of other related patent documents (such as those found through a prior art search) likely also thought the same. As such, to address infringement concerns, it makes sense for an inventor to review the claims of the relevant prior art patent documents uncovered during the novelty search. Although the prior art search does not answer the question of whether one may *properly* make, sell, or offer the invention, or import the invention into, the United States without infringement liabilities, it does provide a small measure of assurance that making and marketing the invention does not infringe on another's patent, at least those found during the novelty search. You need to ask for this to be done because it is not normally performed. Please be aware that such searches and reviews only minimally mitigate the possibility of patent infringement liability and do not eliminate it.

When to forgo a novelty search

The value of a novelty search is diminished if the inventor is committed to launching the product regardless of whether there is a likelihood that a patent will be granted on the invention. The purpose of the novelty search is to determine whether the inventor will decide to file a patent application and more consequentially, *if he or she will launch* the product in the marketplace. If the inventor plans to launch the product regardless of the result of the novelty search (i.e., even if the novelty search renders a negative opinion), it may be better to forgo the novelty search and use those funds to prepare and file a patent application.

Here is the reasoning: the novelty search is about one-third to one-fourth of the cost of a patent application and is likely significantly less than the cost to launch a business or product. If an inventor uses the novelty search to decide whether to launch the product or business and whether to file a patent application, the novelty search would be beneficial. This is because it could save the inventor a significant amount of time and money. However, if an inventor only wishes to use the novelty search to decide whether to file the patent application and nevertheless plans to launch a business regardless of a negative opinion based on the novelty search, it may be beneficial to forgo the novelty search and redirect these funds toward preparing and filing the patent application.

Another reason that an inventor may wish to forgo a novelty search is if he or she has already invested a substantial amount of time and money in the research and development of an invention (i.e., has incurred a sunk cost). Once again, in this scenario, the inventor is committed to launching the product, and forgoing the novelty search and applying the funds to the patent application process may be a better use of limited funds.

Filing a patent application to protect a revenue stream, even if you forgo the novelty search

Patents have many purposes including the primary function of protecting the revenue stream generated by future sales of the patented or patent pending product or method. The decision to spend money and time to seek the patent should typically occur before the start of any sales or marketing. Although the patent application can be filed after the start of marketing, that is generally not recommended. Postponing the filing of the application until after the start of marketing efforts jeopardizes one's ability to secure a patent because a third-party may file its own patent application before the inventor (see Chapter 5).

If the novelty search is bypassed, it may still be preferable to incur the cost to prepare and file the patent application. It is understandable that inventors only want to spend money on legal fees when necessary or when the issuance of a patent is likely. But, it is worth *preserving* the option to seek patent protection later on in case the product does well in the marketplace. At that time, the inventor can vigorously pursue the patent so that large corporations can be excluded from making, using, selling, or offering the patented invention for sale or importing the invention to the United States. If the inventor does not want to spend a lot of money, there are cost-saving strategies for securing a patent.

Side Note: to preserve the option to secure a patent, a patent application should be filed. If the inventor files a patent application and the product does not do well on the market, the patent application can be abandoned. But if the product does do well on the market, the inventor can speed up examination of the patent application to secure the patent faster. This is a cost-effective strategy that has helped many of my clients work through this issue. If a patent application is not filed, you cannot get a patent in the future. Your own offer for sale of the inventive product become prior art against your own patent application after one year (See one-year grace period in Chapter 5).

First, to secure a patent, there are two major costs: preparing and filing the patent application (i.e., patent preparation costs) and responding to office actions from the USPTO (i.e., patent examination costs). To lower costs associated with the patent preparation, an inventor can file a "provisional application." A provisional patent application costs less than a non-provisional application because it has fewer required sections. Moreover, a provisional patent application is never examined and remains pending for twelve months. Thus, patent examination costs are not incurred. The benefit of filing a provisional patent application is that an inventor is able to secure patent pendency for a period of twelve months and thus delay the patent examination costs for at least twelve months.

If the product does well in the first twelve months after filing the provisional application, the inventor can file a nonprovisional application with a prioritized examination request before the twelve-month period is over to speed up examination. This request moves the patent application to the front of the queue and the application is typically examined within six months. If the invention has not been successful in the marketplace, the inventor can abandon the provisional application and forego filing a corresponding nonprovisional application. This will end the invention's status of patent pendency. If the inventor is still undecided as to whether the invention might be successful in the marketplace, he or she can file the corresponding nonprovisional application within the twelve-month period claiming priority back to the provisional application to maintain patent pendency on the invention. "Claiming priority" is a statement or assertion in the later filed nonprovisional patent application referencing the earlier filed provisional patent application. Claiming priority allows the subject matter of the nonprovisional patent application to be considered as if it were applied for on the filing date of the earlier filed provisional patent application. The nonprovisional application could be filed without the prioritized examination request. If so, the nonprovisional application will usually be taken up for examination in fourteen months to three years, and during this time, the inventor can enjoy the benefits of patent pendency as well as delayed patent examination costs.

CHAPTER 4

Core Concept 4:
Different Ways to Protect an Idea

The main problem that I see with inventors is when they want to use the cheapest form of Intellectual Property (IP) protection. Inventors need to realize that each form (i.e., patents, trademarks, trade secrets and copyright) protects an idea in a different way and is used for a different purpose. It is important to not cut corners and settle for any form of IP protection but rather to get the form of IP protection that best suits the inventor's need. Otherwise, the inventor will not be able to stop others from competing against them.

There are four main types of intellectual property rights that can be secured to protect an idea, invention, proprietary information, or work of art, and each type of protection provides coverage differently. In this chapter, a brief overview of trade secrets, trademarks, and copyrights as well as an extensive treatment of utility and design patents are discussed.

Most products can be protected by multiple types of intellectual property rights. Take, for example, a can of Coca-Cola®. The brand, "Coca-Cola," is a trademark. The formula for the actual soda is a trade secret, while copyright protects the packaging art. The shape of the Coca-Cola® bottle is protected by both (1) a design patent and (2) a trademark (i.e., trade dress). Accordingly, it is important to parse out which aspects of the invention or idea are suitable for patent protection, trademark protection, or copyright protection and which aspects of the invention or idea should be protected by trade secrets.

　　Table 1 below offers a simplified way of remembering each type of protection and what it protects.

Trade Secrets	... **protect...**	Information
Trademarks	... **protect...**	Brands
Copyrights	... **protect...**	Creativity
Patents (utility and design)	... **protect...**	Inventions

Table 1

Trade secrets

A "trade secret" includes any valuable information that is not publicly known and for which the owner has taken, "reasonable"[5] steps to maintain its secrecy. Trade secrets are not registered with a governmental body. Rather, their owner must prove in court when suing someone for trade secret misappropriation that the information fits the definition of a trade secret, given above. Trade secret protection lasts until the information is no longer valuable, the information is not secret, or the owner does not take reasonable steps to maintain its secrecy.

　　Table 2 below delineates each type of protection and the major differences between them.

Type of Protection	Subject Matter	Duration of Protection	Registration Process
Trade Secrets	Valuable Business Information	Indefinite	No
Trademark	Brand	Indefinite	Yes/No
Copyright	Works of Authorship	¯100 years	Yes/No
Utility Patent	Useful Inventions	20 years	Yes
Design Patent	Ornamental Features	15 years	Yes

Table 2

Trade secret law specifically protects the misappropriation of trade secret information. This means that a wrongful or nefarious act must accompany the acquisition of the information. For example, if someone acting as an imposter *steals* the trade secret information from its owner, the owner can sue the imposter for misappropriation of trade secrets. However, if the owner *voluntarily gives* trade secret information to an individual without limitation, there has been no misappropriation and the owner cannot sue. It is also possible that the information may lose its status as a trade secret. This can occur if there has been a lack of reasonable effort to keep the information secret and/or the information is *de facto* no longer a secret.

Trade secret protection is not appropriate in the long term for ideas that can be readily ascertained by reverse engineering or for inventions that can be independently created because, again, if there is no nefarious act that accompanies the acquisition of the information, there is generally no misappropriation or wrongful appropriation of the trade secret information.

Trade secret protection may be optimal for ideas and inventions that can be used secretly and cannot be reverse engineered (e.g., recipes). Generally, trade secret protection is not optimal for mechanical or software products since both utilize a user interface that is available to the public and can therefore be reverse engineered. Most inventions start off as trade secrets. Inventors are often initially hesitant to reveal their inventions to others, including their patent attorney, and I respect their attempts to maintain the secrecy of their inventions.

Besides the invention itself, other aspects related to the business may be protected as trade secrets. For example, the business plan and computer-aided drawings of the invention (including, but not limited to, its tolerances and critical-sizing aspects) may not be eligible for patent protection but may be protected by trade secret. However, the invention will eventually be marketed and will no longer be a trade secret. As such, other forms of intellectual property (i.e., trademarks, copyrights, and patents) should be filed so that competitors do not copy the idea without authorization.

Trademarks

Trademarks protect brands. The inventor may have a name that will be associated with the product or a service mark associated with a service, which are called trademarks. Since the laws for both trademarks and service marks are similar, I will refer to all the above as products and their trademarks for simplicity. A trademark is anything by which customers can identify the product or the source of the product, such as a name associated with the product. Other source identifiers that can be protected by a trademark include sounds, colors, smells, and anything else that can bring the product and/ or its owner to the minds of a consumer. The most common types of trademarks are word-marks, logos, and slogans. If the product configuration (e.g., shape of Coca-Cola® bottle) or packaging (e.g., Tiffany's blue packaging) are nonfunctional and recall the product's maker (i.e., source of the product) in the mind of consumers, the configuration can be protected and registered as a trademark.

The order in which trademark protection should be sought begins first with the wordmark, then the stylized words, logos, and slogans. The wordmark refers to a word, or set of words, associated with a product that does not have a design element attached to it (i.e., standard character mark). If the wordmark is registered without reference to the design elements, infringement would occur even if a competitor used a different design element but still used the same wordmark. The wordmark is the most important trademark registration to secure because competitors tend to infringe on, or copy, the words of the wordmark and not the design elements associated with the wordmark. This is especially common in the current online and text-based world. It is therefore usually a priority to protect the plain wordmark with a trademark registration before the stylized version of the wordmark, slogans, or logos (but if additional funds are available, one can file additional trademark applications for the wordmark with design).

Trademark rights can be acquired by using it in commerce. Sales of the product or service give the seller or manufacturer the right to claim ownership of trademark rights of the wordmark. These are granted based on "common law trademark rights." Common law trademark rights are acquired by operation of law without any registration process. The problem with relying on such rights is that the trademark owner must prove ownership of the mark in a court of law if the trademark owner wishes to sue for trademark infringement. This can be difficult to do, and the burden is on the trademark owner to retrieve old records of sales, advertisements, and whatever else may be needed to prove ownership based on common law trademark rights. With federal or state trademark registration, the registration certificate (see Appendix D) shows *prima facie* (accepted as correct until proven otherwise) evidence of trademark ownership in the mark.

Although not required, it is beneficial to register a federal trademark with the USPTO when starting a business or launching a product because, as *prima facie* evidence of the registrant's ownership of the mark, it establishes validity of the registered mark as well as exclusive rights to use it in commerce. Moreover, registration allows the trademark owner to slowly expand geographical use of the mark. For example, if the trademark is not registered and the trademark owner uses the mark commercially only in California, the trademark owner has no trademark rights in other states unless the trademark owner uses the mark commercially in those other states. With a federal trademark registration, trademark protection extends throughout the United States and its territories as of the filing date of an application regardless of the extent of its actual geographical use and given the trademark application matures into a federal trademark registration. Trademarks can also be protected by a state trademark registration process through the Secretary of State. However, state trademark rights provide protection only throughout the state where the trademark is registered and not throughout the entire United States.

Trademark rights last until the trademark owner abandons the trademark rights. To find out more information about trademarks and their registration process, see Appendix A.

Copyrights

Copyrights protect original works of authorship that are fixed in a "tangible medium of expression." This means that the authored or creative work has been written down on a piece of paper, saved on an electronic storage device (e.g., hard drive, flash drive), or preserved in some other tangible format. Examples of copyrightable works include movies, videos, photos, books, diaries, articles, and software. Copyright does not protect ideas or useful items, which is the function of patents. Although software is a functional item, it can be protected by copyrights due to the creativity in the selection, ordering, and arrangement of the various pieces of code in the software.

Copyright law does not protect functional features of products such as the mechanical clicker mechanism as discussed in Chapter 1. In fact, when a functional feature is integrated with an aesthetic design, the aesthetic design may not be protected by copyright. For example, if there are aesthetic design elements of a belt buckle, they may not be protectable by copyright because the aesthetic elements are said to be fused with the functional feature. However, it could be protected by a design patent (discussed below), which is not limited in this way.

Authored works are automatically copyrighted at the time they are fixed in a tangible medium of expression. For any work created on, or after, January 1, 1978, the term of copyright protection is the entirety of the author's life plus seventy years after the author's death. For works made for hire as well as anonymous and pseudonymous works, the duration of copyright is ninety-five years from publication or 120 years from creation, whichever is shorter.

Registration is not required, but is advantageous to secure. If a copyright application is filed within three months of its publication or prior to the start of infringement, the copyright owner may seek statutory damages of up to 150,000 dollars in federal court, plus attorney's fees, from the infringer. This often makes litigation financially unattractive for the copyright *infringer*. Without copyright registration, each party pays their own attorney's fees and the damages are limited to actual damages, which may be significantly less than statutory damages. This often makes litigation financially unattractive for the copyright *owner*.

Patents

Three types of patents may be registered: utility, design, and plant patents. Plant patents are directed to asexually reproducing plants. Since this is a highly-specialized topic, it will not be covered below.[6] If the invention is described in terms of its function or utility, a utility patent application would be the best type of protection. Utility patents protect inventions encompassing new functional features incorporated into an existing product or a new functional product as well as novel methods (for example, manufacturing techniques). If the invention is described in terms of its aesthetics, a design patent application would be the best type of protection. The design patent application protects the ornamentation, sculpture, pattern design, layout, and other aesthetic features of a product.

It is possible for one product to qualify for multiple types of intellectual property protection, and "stacking" them may be useful.

For example, a Coca-Cola bottle can be protected with multiple intellectual property rights. The shape of the bottle can function as a trademark, which is referred to as the trade dress. In addition to qualifying for trade dress trademark protection, the product's shape can also qualify for design patent protection. The printed design on the bottle qualifies for copyright protection. Also, the technology used to make the bottle can qualify for utility patent protection. Applying for multiple intellectual property rights on one product may provide comprehensive protection. However, if funds are limited, it may be best to seek the type of intellectual property rights that best match the product.

Strategy for utility patent protection

The recommended strategy for protecting an invention with a provisional or nonprovisional utility patent may depend on a number of factors. For example, the funds that the inventor is willing to invest, the importance of having an issued patent rather than patent pendency, and the developmental stage of the product. Although other factors exist, these three generally dictate whether a provisional or nonprovisional utility patent application should be filed. To understand how these three factors might change the strategies for patent protection, a brief introduction to provisional and nonprovisional applications is necessary.

Provisional and nonprovisional utility patent applications

Utility patent applications can be filed as provisional patent applications or nonprovisional applications. The primary difference between the two is that the provisional application merely establishes a priority date (i.e., filing date) for the subject matter it discloses.

If two inventors file separate applications for the same invention, the one who filed first is given priority over the second when granting the patent. If nothing is done after filing the provisional patent application, it will be abandoned twelve months later and the information about the invention contained in the provisional patent application will no longer be patent pending. To maintain pendency on the information or priority for the filing date of the provisional application, the inventor must file a nonprovisional application within the twelve-month period and claim priority back to the provisional patent application.

The nonprovisional application similarly serves to establish a priority date for the subject matter disclosed. However, a nonprovisional application also enters a queue for examination. The nonprovisional application is only abandoned if a patent applicant fails to submit a response to an office action made by the USPTO. Any subject matter shared by the nonprovisional patent application and the provisional patent application will have the same priority date. (For more detailed information about provisional and nonprovisional applications, see Section 2.)

Strategic Factor 1 for utility patent protection: monetary funds

The provisional patent application is a lower-cost option for filing a patent application. As such, if cost is an important factor, a provisional patent application should be filed instead of a nonprovisional application to minimize legal costs. As explained above, it is important to remember that the provisional patent application only secures patent pendency of the inventor's idea for twelve months. A provisional application does not enter the queue for examination and does not provide any enforceable patent rights that can be used to sue another for damages or seek an injunction.

Strategic Factor 2 for utility patent protection: time frame for securing a patent

The provisional patent application can also be utilized to delay the expenses of the patent application examination. As stated above, a provisional patent application does not enter the queue for examination and is automatically abandoned twelve months after its filing.

If the inventor primarily seeks patent pendency rather than the issuance of the patent, a provisional patent application can initially be filed to delay the application from entering the queue for examination for up to twelve months, which in turn delays examination costs by twelve months.

However, if the ability to assert a claim against others or show potential licensees what has been protected is important to the inventor, the nonprovisional patent application should be filed instead of the provisional utility patent application. This way the patent application will enter the queue for examination as soon as possible. After the nonprovisional patent application is filed and enters the queue for examination, the USPTO examines the patent application on a first come, first served basis (see Chapter 7). It normally takes one to three years for the inventor to receive the first office action from the USPTO.

If an inventor does not want to wait that long, he or she may file the application along with a prioritized examination request for an additional fee. This typically reduces the wait time for the first office action to roughly six months.

In sum, the provisional patent application and the prioritized examination request make the timeline of a patent application process more flexible. They can be utilized to design a shorter or longer time frame that is more suitable for the inventor's manufacturing and marketing time table.

Strategic Factor 3 for utility patent protection: development stage of the product

It may be better to file a provisional utility patent application instead of a nonprovisional application if the idea or point of novelty is not yet fully developed. However, for inventions that have a clearly defined point of novelty, an inventor may consider filing the nonprovisional application to have the invention examined by the USPTO for patentability. If an inventor has built a prototype and conducted sufficient tests that satisfactorily prove its functionality (i.e., proof of concept) and marketability, he or she may wish to file the nonprovisional application *and* enter the queue for examination on the invention.

The provisional patent application is more suitable for less developed ideas because it allows the inventor to alter and include additional information in the patent application before examination by the USPTO. The provisional application should include a description of the invention up to its current point of development. The inventor then has twelve months to further develop the idea, build prototypes, and test functionality. Before the twelve-month period expires, the nonprovisional application must be filed with priority claimed back to the provisional application. The inventor may add information learned during the twelve-month period in the nonprovisional application. It is important to note that only the original information in the provisional patent application receives priority of the filing date of the provisional patent application. The new information (added when filing the nonprovisional application) receives a priority date of the filing date of that nonprovisional patent application.

It is also possible to file multiple provisional applications with improvements as the inventor develops the product during that twelve- month period. At the end of this period, all additional information contained in these various provisional applications is filed collectively in one nonprovisional application. In this way, only one nonprovisional patent application ultimately enters the queue for examination. The benefit of doing this is that the inventor avoids separate, nonprovisional applications and avoids unnecessary costs of multiple nonprovisional patent applications.

Even if the ideas for a utility patent are fully developed and the product is ready for marketing, the inventor may still benefit from filing a provisional application because it delays examination. After filing the provisional application, the inventor may test the invention in the market. This testing period may clarify the importance of certain features or evince problems of the original version of the product. The inventor may then include this new information in the nonprovisional application when it is later filed. The information added to the patent application should be directly related to the point of novelty to warrant the expense of an attorney's time to amend the patent application. In this way, the provisional application provides flexibility and control in what will ultimately be examined by the USPTO for patentability.

Side Note: I have insisted that correctly identifying the point of novelty is essential for determining the types of intellectual property used to protect the invention, drafting the patent application, and prosecuting the patent application before the USPTO. However, one should not cling too tightly to a specific point of novelty. If during research, development, or marketing, the inventor feels that the original point of novelty has changed or is already known, the strategy in prosecuting and securing the patent should also be adjusted according to that new information.

Strategy for design patent protection

Design patent applications protect ornamental features, unique design elements, or patterns of a product. The term for design patents is fifteen years upon the issuance of a design patent, whereas the term of a utility patent is twenty years upon filing. Unlike the straightforward patent term calculation for design patents, the patent term for utility patents is more complicated to calculate because it is contingent on (including, but not limited to): the filing of a provisional application, payment of maintenance fees, patent term adjustments, terminal disclaimers, etc. Design patent applications generally have a higher "allowance rate" than that of utility patent applications—a higher number of design patent applications mature into a patent compared to utility patent applications. However, because design patent applications protect the ornamentation and not the function of an invention, competitors can easily avoid infringing on design patents than utility patents by simply making their products look different. Design protections are therefore only useful in limited situations. However, limited usefulness does not necessitate ignoring them. Below are a few situations in which a design patent may prove very useful.

Situation 1: to block importation of overseas manufacturer overruns

Design patents are useful for blocking the sale of counterfeits, the importation of overrun (i.e., excess production), or rejected products manufactured overseas for the inventor. These imports will be identical to the drawings in the design patent and, if imported into the United States, may be blocked by Customs. If these products are allowed into the United States, the importers, distributors, users, or manufacturers may be sued for infringement.

Situation 2: furniture

Design patents are also useful for furniture lines and other products sold in sets because buyers must purchase products that look like the original product to maintain complete sets. Doing otherwise would create aesthetically displeasing groupings of products that a potential consumer would not be interested in when expanding their current set.

Situation 3: large market leaders

Design patents may also be useful for large manufacturers that are leaders in their market. For example, Apple, Inc. obtained several design patents on different parts of its iPhone including the housing and arrangement of icons on the display. Apple, Inc. won a lawsuit against Samsung for design patent infringement when Samsung put out its own version of a smartphone with a similar design in the United States.

CHAPTER 5

Core Concept 5:
Three Bars to Patentability and the First-Inventor-to- File Regime

Inventors may want to market their invention first and file the patent application later to save money on legal fees. This plan, however, is problematic. If, for example, a third party files a patent application before the inventor or publicly markets the same product, the inventor would be prevented from being able to secure a patent at all. Moreover, it is possible that the inventor would discover this much later after having invested a substantial sum of time and money, which would go to waste because the third party would be awarded the patent, not you.

There are three bars to patentability: public use, printed publication, and offer for sale (see Figure 2 below). Bars to patentability specify the conditions under which the one-year time period begins before the inventor must file a patent application or be barred from seeking patent protection forever. These conditions are often associated with marketing efforts of the product.

One-year personal grace period

Before I explain each of the bars to patentability in detail, it is important to understand why I call the "one-year grace period" the "one-year personal grace period." U.S. patent laws permit inventors to publicly use, offer for sale, and distribute a printed publication of their invention for one year before the inventor must file the patent application. The inventor does not need to file a patent application before marketing the product, but may legally wait up to one year after the start of marketing efforts before filing the patent application. If an application is not filed within one year of starting marketing efforts, the inventor is barred forever from seeking patent protection.

Taking advantage of the one-year grace period is not recommended. Although nothing the inventor does *personally* during that one-year period will bar the inventor from seeking a patent on the invention, the same is not true for the actions of a third-party. If *a third-party* gives a public demonstration, makes an offer for sale, distributes a printed publication, or files a patent application related to the invention before the inventor files his or her own patent application with the USPTO, the third-party's actions would be considered prior art and may invalidate the inventor's patent, as will be discussed below in the section entitled "First-Inventor-to-File Regime." This is true even if the third-party saw the inventor's invention and copied it. The inventor may have recourse against the third-party, but such recourse would require an expenditure of time and money. The unpredictable nature of litigation and related costs would make seeking such redress economically infeasible. Hence, the one-year grace period should be treated as being solely personal to the inventor and not necessarily beneficial for the inventor because the one-year grace period does not protect you against the actions of a third-party.

Bars to Patentability

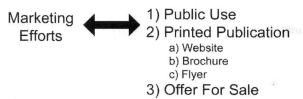

Marketing
Efforts
1) Public Use
2) Printed Publication
   a) Website
   b) Brochure
   c) Flyer
3) Offer For Sale

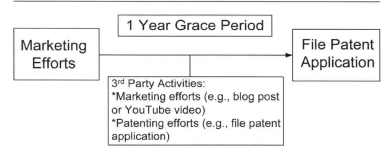

Figure 2

The Three Bars to Patentability: Public use, printed publication, and offer for sale

Public Use

"Public use" includes any use of the invention where the public has access to such use. Non-public uses may be considered public use even if no one is around to see the product being used. For example, use of an invention by a person who is not under any limitation, restriction, or obligation of secrecy to the inventor would be considered a public use even if the use was behind closed doors.

For example, in the case *New Railhead Manufacturing LLC v. Vermeer Manufacturing Co.*[7] New Railhead, the patent owner, sued Vermeer for patent infringement of a drill bit and a method of using the bit to drill rock formations. As part of the proceedings, the court considered the types of uses that New Railhead (the patent owner) had engaged in more than one year before the filing of its patent application that could have been considered a public use. The court considered New Railhead's drill bit and method of using the bit to drill rock formations to be in public use even though it was used underground and out of plain sight, and they lost the case. The result of this case means that even if an invention is used where it cannot be seen by others (i.e., not openly in public), the invention may still be considered in public use. Inventors should bear in mind that even if an invention's use is not visible to the public, it could still be considered public.

The "experimental use" exception is an exception to the public use bar. It applies when the invention is still being tested and use of the invention in public may be necessary to properly test its functionality. However, once proof of concept has been established through testing, experimentation should stop. Otherwise, any continued use may cease to qualify as "experimental use" and constitute public use, which would bar the inventor from securing the patent if the public use occurred for more than one year before the filing of the patent application. Even if an inventor is using the invention for experimental purposes, he or she should still submit a patent application within one year of starting any public use because it is difficult to know when the exception no longer applies. By filing within one year of the start of use (even experimental), the inventor may avoid potential attacks on the validity of the patent based on whether a use is a public or experimental.

Printed Publication

A "printed publication" is a physical or electronic document that is indexed, catalogued, and shelved so that it is publicly accessible. In other words, it is any information that is printed on a piece of paper or stored electronically, available to the public, and categorized so that one of ordinary skill could locate such information if interested. Websites, brochures, and flyers are some examples of printed publications. In the past, most legal disputes over whether a document is a printed publication involved thesis papers stored in university libraries. A thesis paper would be considered a printed publication if it was catalogued by subject matter in a way that the public could access it. Currently, most issues related to whether a document is a printed publication involve online publications, such as online forums. The same general standard discussed above applies.

Offer for Sale

An "offer for sale" is an offer from an inventor to another person or entity to purchase a product embodying the invention. Even if the potential buyer does not accept the offer, it still qualifies as an offer for sale.

The following is counterintuitive. Even if an offer is not from an inventor *to* another person or entity, it may nonetheless be considered an offer for sale. For example, once the invention has moved out of the experimentation stage, the inventor may outsource its manufacturing and place an order for a production run. The contract from the third-party manufacturing vendor to the inventor may be considered an offer for sale.

In highly contested litigation, the dates on such purchase orders may be determinative as to whether a patent is valid or invalid. In *Hamilton v. Sunbeam*,[8] the patent owner (Hamilton) sued the accused infringer (Sunbeam) for patent infringement of its slow cooker. It was discovered that Hamilton had issued a purchase order to its manufacturing vendor to build its slow cooker more than one year before Hamilton had submitted a patent application. In response to the purchase order, the manufacturing vendor indicated that it was ready to start the manufacturing process and therefore ready to sell the units to the patent holder (i.e., Hamilton). For the court, this constituted an offer of sale and Hamilton lost the case to Sunbeam because Hamilton did not file a patent application less than one year before the offer for sale date (i.e., date of the purchase order from the manufacturer).

Hamilton was not commercializing the invention in the normal sense of making a profit from consumers. However, because Hamilton had ordered units to sell them to the general public, and the manufacturing vendor was ready to sell the units to the patentee, the courts characterized the contract from the manufacturing vendor to the inventor as an offer to sell. The court ruled that this triggered the one- year period in which the inventor needed to file the corresponding patent application. Hamilton lost because the patent application for the slow cooker was filed over a year after ordering units from the manufacturer for sale.

Therefore, it is important to keep track of any "offers of sale" including the dates of manufacturing contracts for the invention, and to file a patent application within one year of any such transaction to avoid this bar of patentability.

Side Note: Another risk of using the one-year personal grace period is the potential waiver of foreign patent protection or loss of ability to seek a patent in foreign countries. As will be discussed in Chapter 6, many foreign countries require what is known as "absolute novelty," which requires the inventor to initiate marketing efforts *after* filing the patent application. The United States is a "relative novelty" country, because U.S. patent laws allow for public disclosure of the invention through marketing efforts for a limited, one-year period *before* the patent application must be filed.

First-inventor-to-file regime

The "first-inventor-to-file regime" dictates that the first inventor to file a patent application with the USPTO is awarded the patent regardless of who was the first to invent or conceive of the invention. The rules of the first-inventor-to-file regime (FITF) must be understood in conjunction with the one- year personal grace period because the FITF rules greatly reduce any benefit of using the one-year personal grace period.

The one-year personal grace period does not protect you against a third party that *files a patent application* on the same or similar idea as your invention. Under the FITF rules, they would be awarded the patent, not you. This was not the case under the prior first-to-invent regime.

Third parties can also interfere with the original inventor's ability to secure a patent by engaging in *marketing efforts* before the original inventor has submitted a patent application (see Figure 2). This is true even if the third party's activities are based on the inventor's information. Any public use, offer for sale, or printed publication by a third-party that occurs prior to the filing of the original inventor's patent application is considered prior art and bars the original inventor from securing a patent. A third party's marketing effort that occur during the original inventor's one-year grace period before the inventor files a patent application can therefore bar the original inventor from patenting his or her invention.

An inventor risks third-party interference if he or she markets an invention during the one-year grace period before filing the patent application. The third-party may observe the inventor's marketing efforts and file their own patent application first. The first-inventor-to-file regime does not take into consideration the date of an inventor's conception. Instead, the USPTO only consider the filing dates of the patent applications when issuing a patent. Although there may be some recourse against a third-party that submits a patent application on another inventor's product, such recourse may be expensive to prove and the outcome unpredictable. Therefore, most inventors do not seek such recourse and instead would most likely quit marketing and selling their product to avoid patent infringement liability.

Continuing any marketing or selling of one's product after a third-party has submitted a patent application risks infringing on the patent rights of the first-to-file inventor if, and when, the patent application matures into a patent. The inventor may believe he or she is protected by a marketing date (e.g., public use, offer for sale, or printed publication) that falls prior to the filing date of the third-party's patent application and that the inventor's marketing would invalidate the third-party's patent. However, in practice, patent litigation would not occur until many years later and the inventor would have to prove that his or her marketing efforts constitute prior art that invalidates the third-party's patent. This may seem relatively easy, but over the course of years memories fade, documents are lost, and the ability of the inventor to provide prior use evidence may be difficult or impossible. The bottom line is that the original inventor has to deal with an issued patent owned by a third-party. Any litigation based on the third-party's patent must still be addressed and will cost time and money.

One form of recourse is a derivation proceeding in which the inventor must prove that the third-party inventor (i.e., first to file inventor) derived their patented invention from the "first" inventor. If successful, the "first" inventor is awarded the patent instead of the third-party that filed first. However, a stringent reading of the law appears to require the "first" inventor to prove there was a chain of communication with the third-party by which the third-party derived the invention from the original inventor. This chain of communication is difficult to prove, especially when sufficient documentation of marketing efforts may be lacking.

CHAPTER 6

Core Concept 6:
Preserving Foreign Patent Protection

Foreign protection is recommended if there is a concrete pathway to monetize the invention in foreign markets. For example, global corporations often have established marketing channels to seek foreign patent protection and the potential for future revenues justifies the expenses. However, it is often difficult for solo inventors and startups to make money abroad. In this case, foreign patent protection may not be fruitful for solo inventors and startups. Nevertheless, one reason to pursue foreign patent protection is that potential licensees or future buyers might want to file in foreign countries. In this case, filing a Patent Cooperation Treaty (PCT) application may make sense to further preserve an inventor's ability to file a patent application in foreign countries later.

Foreign patent protection is an intricate process. It requires significant funds to file a patent application in a foreign country and secure the patent and often makes more sense for larger companies with established business relationships and distribution networks in foreign countries. For multinational companies, the countries in which foreign patent protection should be sought is known and can be projected with reasonable accuracy, which is often not the case for startups and solo inventors. For solo inventors and startups, I generally do not advocate that they seek foreign patent protection without a good reason to do so.

If a large corporation, solo inventor, or startup wants to secure foreign patent protection, *preserving* the right to file in foreign countries later on is not cost prohibitive and it may be beneficial. Future investors and licensees may find a patent portfolio more desirable if there is a still a right to file patent applications in foreign countries. The following discussion explains one strategy for seeking foreign patent protection. Although there are many ways to acquire foreign patent protection, most inventors go through the following process.

Relative novelty versus absolute novelty

Most foreign countries require "absolute novelty" (i.e., marketing efforts for the invention start *after* filing a patent application) of an invention if foreign protection is to be sought. In contrast to "absolute novelty" countries, the United States is a "relative novelty" country because, by utilizing the one-year grace period, inventors can commercialize the invention for up to one year *before* the patent application must be filed. In other words, the invention is not "absolutely," but only "relatively" novel at the time of filing due to the inventor's own marketing efforts. If marketing efforts are conducted before filing the patent application, foreign patent protection is generally waived (see Waive Foreign Protection in Figure 3).

To secure foreign patent protection, an inventor should file a patent application *prior* to marketing efforts, which ensures absolute novelty of the invention. The filing of a U.S. patent application preserves, by treaty (i.e., agreement) with foreign countries, the inventor's ability to file a patent application in foreign countries and claim priority back to the filing of the U.S. patent application within certain statutory timelines (see Figure 3). The marketing efforts done prior to the filing of the foreign patent application, which would normally destroy absolute novelty, are not counted against the later-filed foreign patent application when a foreign patent application is filed based on the previously filed U.S. patent application. This course of action falls in line with recommendations from Chapter 5 (i.e., file patent application before marketing) and avoids any issue related to third-party actions that might block an inventor's ability to secure patent protection in the United States under the first-inventor-to-file regime.

Foreign Protection

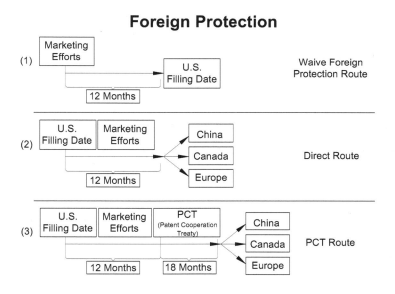

Figure 3

Three foreign protection routes are (1) waive foreign patent protection, (2) maintain absolute novelty and file patent applications within twelve months in specific foreign countries, and (3) maintain absolute novelty, file a PCT application, and enter the national stage after thirty months.

Patent cooperation treaty (PCT) application

After filing a patent application in the United States, the inventor has twelve months (see Direct Route in Figure 3) to decide in which countries or regions to file an application for patent. The twelve-month period begins on the date of the first-filed patent application within the chain of priority, whether a provisional or nonprovisional application. An inventor may file a patent application directly in each country, though for many, this is cost prohibitive. Filing a patent application in Canada, for example, may cost about 2,000 dollars, while filing a patent application in Europe may cost an additional 8,000 dollars. The cost will likely be particularly burdensome if there are multiple countries in which the inventor wants to protect the invention. The cost may not be worthwhile if the inventor's knowledge of the market is unclear. Twelve months is a relatively short period of time to market a product and many inventors do not know where it would be best to seek foreign patent protection. Fortunately, there is a way to further delay filing in specific countries. An inventor can choose to file a PCT application within twelve months after filing the U.S. patent application (provisional or nonprovisional). (See PCT Route in Figure 3).

When the PCT application is filed, this is referred to as "entering the international stage," or the part of the process before filing one or more country specific patent applications. Although the PCT is referred to as an "application" and it is examined, the predominant function of the PCT application is an extension of time that delays the due date when a country specific patent application must be filed. The application enters the "national stage" when the patent application is filed in that country. In other words, filing the PCT application delays for eighteen months the due date for filing a patent application in a specific country (see Figure 3). Instead of having to decide after twelve months where to file, an inventor would have thirty months (i.e., twelve plus eighteen months) after filing of a U.S. patent application to decide in which countries or regions to seek patent protection.

For startups, smaller companies, and solo inventors, I recommend a PCT application to preserve the ability of the inventor to file in foreign countries if there is a good reason to do so. Future buyers or licensees may find that the option to pursue foreign patent protection adds to the value of any deal with the inventor. However, due to the substantial costs of filing and prosecuting a patent application in a foreign country, good reason should exist to justify the expense of filing and pursuing a patent in a country.

Costs and consequences of pursing foreign patent protection

Foreign patent protection is more expensive than patent protection in the United States. One reason is the cost of annuities during the national stage. Many countries require the inventor to pay an annual fee, which ranges from 500 to 3,000 dollars, to maintain the pendency of the patent application in that country. The cost of multiple annuities adds up. Moreover, the annuity only maintains *pendency* of the foreign patent application. It does not grant any enforceable rights that the inventor can assert against third parties. Even after the foreign patent applications mature into patents, maintenance fees or annuities must still be paid to maintain the patent grant.

Declining to pursue foreign patent protection not only avoids costs, but the U.S. patent application can remain confidential until it matures into a patent. Until recently, U.S. patent applications were not published until they matured into a patent, unlike other countries that published patent applications before they were granted. In 2000, the U.S. started to publish patent applications before they were granted to harmonize U.S. patent laws with the laws of many other countries. However, there is one exception to this rule. If, at the time of filing a nonprovisional application, the inventor indicates that he or she does not intend to seek patent protection in foreign countries, the USPTO will not publish upon request the patent application before granting the patent. If the inventor's intent changes before the filing date in foreign countries, the non-publication request can be withdrawn and foreign filing can occur.

The upside to keeping an unpublished U.S. patent application confidential until it matures into a patent is that competitors cannot find out whether the examiner at the USPTO is rejecting the application for patent. For example, if the inventor opts to keep the patent application confidential and the examination is not going well, a third-party cannot know that the inventor is having difficulty in securing patent protection. If a third-party had access to this information, and if prosecution was not proceeding favorable for the inventor, the third-party may feel emboldened to start competing in the marketplace.

The disadvantage of keeping a U.S. patent application confidential is that the patent owner cannot collect damages for infringement that occurred prior to the issue date of the patent. If the patent application is published, however, the inventor can conceivably collect on infringement that occurred since publication, provided the published claims remain substantially the same as the granted claims. This is not common, however, as most claims are amended during examination. Although important to consider, these are not usually sufficient reasons to forgo confidentially in the U.S. application process.

In sum, though it may be a good idea for some solo inventors and startups to preserve the ability to pursue foreign patent protections, I do not generally recommend that they aggressively pursue foreign patent protection in the national stage due to substantial costs and the uncertainty of making money in foreign markets.

CHAPTER 7

Core Concept 7:
The Overall Patent Process and Costs

The patent process is lengthy and may take one to four years to complete. Additionally, the funds spent preparing and filing a patent application are not the only costs involved in securing a patent. There are additional examination costs that should be understood before seeking a patent.

The overall patent process can generally be divided into the cost of preparing and filing the application and the cost of prosecuting a patent application. These are the two major cost centers in securing a patent. The patent prosecution costs include petition fees, costs during the Office Action–Response Cycle, fees for the issuance and maintenance of the patent, fees for submitting an Information Disclosure Statement, and patent attorney fees.

Furthermore, the overall patent process is long and may take years to complete. This chapter will delineate the overall patent process including major costs and the general timeline (see Figure 4 below for a flow chart of the general patent process).

Patent Process

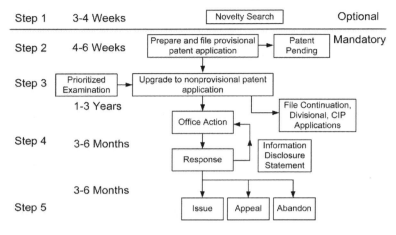

Figure 4

Step 1:
The novelty search

The patent process begins with an optional novelty search. A novelty search is not always recommended. It depends on the inventor's particular situation, as discussed in the section on novelty searches in Chapter 3.

The USPTO does not require the inventor to conduct a search of the prior art to find relevant references. It does, however, impose a duty on inventors to disclose information that is known to the inventors and that is material to the patentability of the invention. Material information is anything that the inventor knows of that might cause an examiner to reject the application for patent. If a novelty search was conducted, the results should be disclosed to the USPTO. The duty to disclose is satisfied by filing an information disclosure statement, discussed in the last section of this chapter.

If a novelty search is conducted and no prior art disclosing the proposed invention's point of novelty is discovered, the next step is to prepare and file a patent application.

Step 2:
Prepare and file a patent application

The preparation and filing of a provisional or nonprovisional patent application may take up to six weeks. Once the patent application is filed, the invention is considered patent pending at which point the inventor may safely disclose or share the invention publicly and begin marketing it.

Side Note: To begin the preparation, a patent attorney and the inventor will discuss the invention. Anything necessary to the understanding of *how* the invention works must be disclosed to the patent attorney. This may include a short-written description and a demonstration of a prototype (not required) of the invention. For me, a one-on-one discussion of the invention and also the background of the inventor and the vision going forward would be needed. This defines the scope of the work to be done. The patent attorney can then provide an accurate price. Before this, any price would be inaccurate. A detailed explanation of the efforts to prepare a patent application is discussed in Section 2.

The patent application may be filed as a provisional or nonprovisional patent application (see Chapter 4 for a summary or Section 2 for a more extensive discussion on provisional and nonprovisional applications). When a provisional application is filed, the invention is patent pending. The provisional patent application is automatically abandoned after twelve months. To avoid abandonment, a corresponding, nonprovisional application must be filed and priority claimed back to the provisional patent application.

Even if the provisional patent application is abandoned, the abandonment of the provisional patent application does not mean that the inventor cannot seek patent protection. For example, if an inventor begins marketing an invention after filing the provisional patent application, and a corresponding nonprovisional application was not filed before the provisional application expired, the inventor loses the ability to seek patent protection only after one year from the start of the marketing efforts, not when the provisional patent application is abandoned. Those marketing efforts would be prior art to any application filed more than one year after the start date of the marketing effort. If an application is filed more than one year after the filing date of the provisional patent application but prior to the one-year anniversary of the start of marketing, the marketing efforts are not prior art to that patent application. The one-year personal grace period, not whether the provisional patent application is abandoned, is the rule that prevents an inventor from securing patent protection. If the provisional application lapses, but the start of marketing efforts occurred less than one year ago, a patent application can still be filed as long as it is within the one-year grace period and as long as the start of marketing efforts do not become prior art to the patent application. Once the one-year grace period has elapsed and the provisional application is abandoned, the inventor is barred from seeking patent protection on the marketed invention.

Side Note: Patent attorneys often use the phrase "patent protection" in two ways, which may confuse inventors. An invention has "patent protection" when it achieves patent pendency status, which is discussed above. Patent pendency establishes the date of invention or the filing date of the patent application with the USPTO. The primary benefit of patent pendency is that third parties are barred from later filing and securing a patent on the same invention (or obvious variants). If an inventor begins marketing the product after filing the patent application, any third-party that files their own patent application based on the marketing efforts of the inventor will have junior rights to the inventor who first filed the patent application. Normally, in a dispute, the inventor who filed first, having "senior rights," would be awarded the patent over the third-party that filed a later patent application. However, if the inventor decided to abandon the patent application, a third-party would have senior rights over other potential parties. This type of patent protection merely refers to patent pendency. No enforceable rights arise out of patent pendency and the inventor would not be able to sue a third-party for infringement until the patent is granted.

An invention also has patent protection when an application matures into an issued patent. An issued patent confers an exclusionary right to the patent owner to stop or exclude others from making, using, selling, or offering their patented product for sale in, or importing to, the United States. This enforceable right enables inventors and businesses to seek damages, royalties, and an injunction on third parties who are infringing on their patent.

Remember, patent attorneys utilize the phrase "patent protection" when speaking of both "patent pendency" and an "issued patent" without clarifying between the two. Be sure to keep this in mind when discussing patent protection with others.

Step 3:
Waiting for a first office action from the USPTO and prioritized examination requests

After filing the patent application, the inventor usually waits one to three years before the USPTO begins an examination of the application for patent. This waiting period can be shortened to three to six months by filing a prioritized examination request and paying an additional fee. The prioritized examination request must be filed *with* the patent application. It cannot be requested after the patent application is filed. However, if an inventor has already filed a patent application without a prioritized examination request but would later like to have the invention examined sooner rather than later, a second nonprovisional application, along with a prioritized examination request claiming priority back to the first nonprovisional application, can be filed.

In lieu of the prioritized examination request, an applicant can also shorten the waiting period for examination by filing a "petition to make special based on age" for expediting examination at any time during patent pendency. This petition does not need to be filed with the patent application. To file this petition, at least one of the inventors must be at least sixty-five years old. If the prioritized examination request or the petition is granted, the patent application is examined out of turn and the first office action will be should be received within five to six months. Put simply, the patent application is pulled from the back of the queue for examination and placed up front. The patent application is not examined on a first-come, first-serve basis but out of turn. The prioritized examination request and the "petition to make special based on age" enable inventors to strategically approach the patent process by shortening the waiting period for the first office action, if and when desired.

Inventors who prefer to delay as much as possible the start of the examination of a patent application may choose to file a provisional application (instead of a nonprovisional patent application), which remains pending for twelve months without any examination. Twelve months after filing the provisional patent application, the inventor may file a corresponding, upgraded, nonprovisional application with a claim of priority back to the provisional patent application. The claim of priority attributes any subject matter disclosed in the nonprovisional application common with the provisional application as if it were filed on the filing date of the original, provisional patent application. If the applicant files a nonprovisional application without a prioritized examination request or a "petition to make special based on age," examination will occur within the normal time-frame of one to three years. By not expediting the examination of the patent application, the patent examination costs associated with the patent process are delayed, and the extra time allows a business to increase revenue before spending more money on patent prosecution. If business picks up and the patent is vital to protecting a revenue stream, another nonprovisional patent application may be filed with the prioritized examination request, or the "petition to make special based on age" may be filed in the current nonprovisional patent application to speed up examination and, ideally, grant of the patent.

This strategy would be advantageous if, for example, a business files a provisional application *after* which demand for the product increases. The inventor could speed up examination to acquire a patent by filing a nonprovisional application during the twelve-month period along with a prioritized examination request or a "petition to make special based on age."

On the other hand, if an issued patent is desired as soon as possible, a nonprovisional application can be filed immediately with a prioritized examination request or a "petition to make special based on age." This would incur prosecution and examination costs earlier but would allow for the application for patent to mature into a patent as soon as possible. The current USPTO system permits flexibility to slow down or speed up the timetable before a patent application undergoes examination.

Step 4:
Office action by the USPTO and
response by the inventor

Once the patent application has been examined by the USPTO, its acceptance or rejection is communicated to the inventor through an "Office Action." An Office Action is simply the official stance of the USPTO—to either reject or to accept the application for patent. Be forewarned: about ninety percent of all patent applications receive an initial Office Action rejection. This occurs by design since the goal is not merely to obtain a patent but to secure a patent with claims that provide sufficiently broad protections against competitors (see Chapter 2) while also avoiding the prior art. After a rejection, the claims can be narrowed slightly and resubmitted to persuade the examiner to allow the application to mature into a patent. Often, a balance needs to be found so that the claims are sufficiently broad yet narrow enough to avoid the prior art and be issued as a patent.

The cost to respond to an Office Action ranges from a few hundred to a few thousand dollars. This "Office Action–Response Cycle" can be repeated indefinitely, but it typically takes one or two cycles to develop an understanding of the examiner's position. A telephone interview with the examiner to better understand his or her position can help expedite the Office Action–Response Cycle and examination process. The telephone interview can occur at any time but is normally conducted after the first office action is received.

Step 5:
Application matures to a patent,
expires, or is abandoned

After the Office Action-Response Cycle(s), the patent application may issue as a patent. Issue fees are due for the patent application to issue as a patent. Maintenance fees are due at three and a half, seven and a half, and eleven and a half years after the issue date. Maintenance fees are collected by the USPTO to generate fees to support the operation of the USPTO. If the maintenance fees are not paid, the patent expires. Hopefully, profits from the sale of the patented product would cover these fees.

If the inventor is not successful in the Office Action-Response Cycle, there are several options to minimize financial expenses. If business is lagging, the inventor may abandon the patent application. Alternatively, the inventor can appeal to the Office Action to the Patent Trademark and Appeal Board (PTAB), which usually takes a long time. The appeal is an administrative proceeding requesting the PTAB to determine whether the examiner's decision is sound. This is a lengthy process and could take one to three years for the PTAB to render an opinion. I would not recommend the appeal process unless progress with the examiner is at a total standstill. Moreover, even if the appeal is won, the application will be remanded back to the same examiner, who can make a new rejection, though that is less likely. The recommended course of action is to work with the examiner as long as possible by addressing the examiner's concerns, amending the claims, and providing arguments in support of patentability.

Information disclosure statement

The duties of candor and good faith are imposed on and require the applicant or anyone prosecuting the patent application (i.e., guiding the patent application through the USPTO) to tell the truth to the USPTO. Throughout the entire application pendency or appeal, the inventor has a duty to disclose material information that an examiner may want to know when determining whether to reject or allow the application to mature into a patent. If there are facts that might cause the USPTO to reject the application, the duties of candor and good faith require the applicant to make the examiner aware of this information. If facts are misstated, the applicant must alert the examiner and correct the facts on the record. Misrepresentations or omissions made with intent to mislead the USPTO on important aspects of the patent examination can make an issued patent unenforceable.

The information should be submitted to the USPTO in the form of an "Information Disclosure Statement" (IDS). The cost to file an IDS may be a few hundred dollars each time the inventor has new information to report. Normally, about one IDS is filed for each patent application.

The IDS form provided by the USPTO is merely a means by which an applicant can *satisfy* his or her duty of candor and good faith in conducting business with the USPTO. It generally contains information regarding prior art references relating to the invention including the results of a novelty search, similar existing technology, offers for sale, printed publications, or public demonstrations of the invention by the inventor that occurred more than one year prior to the filing of the patent application. As discussed in Chapter 5, this information would be relevant to the patentability of the invention and thus, material. If this information is not submitted to the USPTO, it is possible that a breach of the duties of candor and good faith has occurred, which could invalidate the patent if it is granted and if litigation occurs. Please note that the duties of good faith and candor do not require the applicant to *search* the prior art for relevant references. Hence, there is no duty to search the prior art, and the novelty search is an optional step.

It is preferable to submit more information in an IDS, even if it is unclear whether the information is actually material and relevant to patentability of the invention. A significant benefit of disclosing more, rather than less, information relates to the presumption of validity. Information disclosed to the USPTO is added to the file history (i.e., official record) of the patent application. If a patent is issued and relevant information has been disclosed in an IDS, the patent will have a "presumption of validity" over the information submitted in the IDS.

Conversely, if any information is withheld or mischaracterized, potential infringers could allege that the patent is both invalid and unenforceable based on inequitable conduct or breach of the duties of good faith and candor, causing the court to invalidate the patent. The duty to disclose extends to everyone involved in the examination or prosecution of the patent application.

Relevant information that should be presented to the USPTO could be presented in the background section of the patent application. Inclusion in the background section can mitigate a finding of an intent to mislead the examiner and avoid a finding of inequitable conduct. However, any information included in the background section and not in the IDS is not considered to be made of record in the patent application and the patent is not presumed valid over the information. Often, the background section is used to describe prior art when a printed reference is not available. However, because a patent is not presumed valid over the information presented in the background section but *is* presumed valid over information submitted in the IDS, it is preferred to disclose this information in an IDS to enjoy the presumption of validity over such information.

Section 2

Utility and Design Patent Applications

As covered in Chapter 4, the USPTO grants three types of patents: utility, design, and plant patents. The utility patent protects an invention's functional features, while a design patent protects its ornamental features (See Appendix B and Appendix C for sample utility and design patents). Plant patents, which are not covered in this book, protect asexually reproducing plants.

Deciding what application to file: Design or utility?

Utility patents protect an invention's functional aspects but not its aesthetic design. Design patents protect an invention's ornamentation regardless of its functional aspects. The product's point of novelty needs to be deciphered to determine whether it is more appropriate to acquire utility or design patent protection (see Chapter 1 for more information about the point of novelty). If additional funds are available, an inventor may want to seek both. This is beneficial if the invention is only a minor improvement over existing technology (i.e., a "thin invention") or might be novel, but likely considered obvious. By filing for both, the likelihood of receiving some form of protection increases. It is difficult to acquire a utility patent for a thin invention but if the utility patent is more appropriate, it should be sought. A design patent is generally easier to secure and for thin inventions, it may provide some minimal intellectual property protection. Before proceeding with the filing of a design patent application, however, it is important to understand the limitations of design patent protection, some of which are discussed below. Chapter 8 provides a more comprehensive discussion on design patents.

When choosing between a design or utility patent, it may be a useful exercise for the inventor to recall words he or she generally uses to describe the invention. If the description reflects the product's function (e.g., faster, cheaper, easier, etc.,), it is more likely that a utility patent should be sought. If the inventor uses words that describe the invention's aesthetics (e.g., looks, beauty, sleek, etc.,), a design patent should probably be sought.

However, sometimes an inventor's description will encompass both function and aesthetics, for example, building blocks that when assembled constitute an aesthetic product (e.g., a Lego® set). In this case, the ornamentation is not a fixed design but something that can be reconfigured repeatedly. Therefore, the Lego® set's functional features enable one to create something aesthetically pleasing. However, its primary utility is functional. These types of inventions require utility patent protection, because the aesthetic designs are secondary in importance to their functional ability. If the design is fixed and cannot be changed however, the design can be protected by a design patent. However, the inventor ought to understand the limitations of the design patent (see Chapter 8 for a discussion on design patents and below for a discussion on the limitations of design patents).

Some clients prefer to pursue design patents because they are less costly than utility patents. However, they only provide sufficient protection in limited circumstances including, but not limited to, (1) when the product is sold as a set, or a product line shares a unique design element; (2) to ward off lazy competitors and; (3) to prevent manufacturers from selling items that do not pass quality control during manufacturing. Design patent protection may be suitable in other circumstances but the primary ones are discussed below. I will briefly cover each one of these circumstances below.

Unique Design Element

If a business sells a product that is typically sold as a set or if a product line has a common design element (e.g., home goods, furniture, and signage), a design patent may be beneficial. For example, if a customer buys a dining set with four chairs and wants two more, the customer would likely want to purchase chairs of the same design. In another scenario, consumers often prefer to purchase products with a matching design element. For example, if a customer buys an appliance from a given kitchen line, he or she would likely want to purchase kitchen appliances that include the same design element such as matching knobs or handles. If a design patent is not secured on these types of products, competitors would be able to imitate the design and consumers would be able to purchase cheaper, matching, imitation products.

Lazy Competitor

A design patent would also protect against a "lazy competitor." A lazy competitor asks a manufacturer to reverse engineer a product without any significant modification. However, if an inventor has secured a design patent on the product's external appearance, any sales of the reverse engineered product would be identical in design and therefore a clear case of design patent infringement. Design patents force lazy competitors to alter the appearance of their products to avoid liability for design patent infringement. Securing design patents may be a good strategy if the patent owner has had a history, or experience, with such lazy competitors simply copying their products.

Rejected Items from Manufacturing Vendors

Design patents may also prevent the sale of items that did not pass quality control during manufacturing. The manufacturer might try to sell these reject items without the knowledge or authorization of the inventor (a typical problem when manufacturing products in China). Manufacturing overruns (i.e., items manufactured over the ordered amount) are common, and when the inventor does not buy them, the manufacturer may attempt to sell them to third parties to make additional profit on the order. Securing a design patent can deter this conduct since rejected items and overruns would be identical to the design patent and would constitute design patent infringement when sold in or imported into the United States.

How to use this section on patent applications

Inventors should use the information provided in this section to review a patent application *prepared by patent counsel*. It should not be used to prepare a patent application without legal counsel. This section explains the anatomy of a design patent application (Chapter 8) and a utility patent application (Chapters 9- 12), which can be filed as either a provisional or nonprovisional application. Since more utility patents than design patents are sought, most of this section is devoted to utility patent applications. This section also includes tips for helping the inventor review and understand a patent application written by a patent attorney (Chapter 12).

I have rarely seen a *well written* patent application prepared by someone who was not mentored by a senior patent attorney over a period of years. This is one of the reasons that it is my belief that only with proper guidance can an inventor be prepared to write a well-crafted patent application. Nonetheless, some inventors attempt to draft their own patent applications. While I do not advise prosecuting your own patent application, examiners at the USPTO will help *pro se* patent applicants (i.e., inventors that file and prosecute the patent application without the help of a patent attorney) to a limited extent. However, relying upon the help of the USPTO examiner to prosecute a patent application has limited benefits. First, the USPTO is not required to advise the applicant as to the breadth of the claims or whether the claims *suit* the inventor's needs. A patent attorney, however, though not able to *guarantee* the issued patent is sufficiently suitable for your purposes, does help inventors secure patents with claim scopes aligned with their needs, whereas a patent examiner will not. Secondly, an examiner will not help a client secure a *broad* claim, which increases the potential for others to avoid patent infringement liability with a design around. As such, it is highly recommended that patent prosecution be handled by competent patent counsel who can successfully advocate meaningfully broad claims on behalf of the patent applicant and one that is more aligned to your purpose. However, please be advised that retaining a patent attorney to assist you through the patent process does not guarantee a mistake-free patent, but only mitigates potential mistakes.

Again, to avoid complications, I recommend that inventors retain competent patent counsel to prepare and file the patent application, which is an intricate, difficult document to prepare and must comply with numerous government regulations, laws, and case decisions which interpret those laws and regulations. The United States Supreme Court once stated that "the specification [i.e., the actual text and drawings of the patent document] and claims of a patent, particularly if the invention be at all complicated, constitute one of the most difficult legal instruments to draw with accuracy."[9] A patent attorney undergoes years of education and training under the supervision of a senior attorney to become proficient in preparing a patent application. Furthermore, patent attorneys are expected to keep up with current patent case law. Preparing a patent application without professional help risks difficulty and disappointment.

Many complicated legal principles are applicable when drafting a patent application. A self-help book on drafting a patent application may, for example, expose the inventor to these rudimentary principles, but a layperson will have difficulty assimilating these principles with their own writing styles in an application. Mistakes in an application prepared by an inventor may not be noticed until the USPTO's examination has started, or after the patent issues, which might blind side inventors and startups with potential invalidity attacks by defendants.

Inventors should use the information in this book to better understand the patent document, which merges information about the invention and the legal requirements for drafting of a patent application, and to facilitate discussion with patent counsel. Inventors should also use information in this book to double check patent counsel's work. The inventor and attorney cannot, without each other, create an effective patent document.

A patent attorney assimilates the technical details of the invention only after a short discussion with the inventor. Miscommunication may occur and details may not have been conveyed properly or may have been misunderstood. The patent attorney may therefore need clarification regarding the technical details of the invention. Ultimately, inventors should read the draft of the patent application provided by patent counsel thoroughly to be sure that the technical aspects of their invention are correctly described and then bring up any questions they might have with the patent attorney.

CHAPTER 8

Design Applications

Design patents protect the aesthetic design of a product and not its utilitarian features. Inventors are often drawn to a design patent in lieu of a utility patent due to its lower cost. However, seeking a design patent when a utility patent is necessary will not meet the needs of the inventor. Furthermore, though design patent applications are mechanically simple to prepare, they nonetheless require careful attention to detail when preparing the drawings.

The purpose of a design patent application

Design patents are limited in that they protect ornamentation only (e.g., the product appearance). For example, if competitors copy a design or look but make significant enough aesthetic changes, they may avoid design patent infringement liability altogether. Moreover, a design patent is not always necessarily effective for protecting ornamental design in all circumstances (see Introduction to Section 2 for specific circumstances in which a design patent may be useful).

Design patents may not be the proper form of protection because they are easy to circumvent. Changing an invention's appearance could allow the accused infringer to avoid design patent infringement liability. The change must be sufficiently different that an ordinary observer would not confuse the invention shown in the design patent with the accused infringer's design.

By contrast, a utility patent protects the functional aspects of an invention (i.e., its structure or the steps of the patented method), but is not contingent on the design or look of the product for the scope of patent protection it affords. Since design patents and utility patents protect different things, seeking both may be beneficial in certain instances, as discussed in Deciding what application to file: Design or Utility? Section.

The drawings of a design patent application: Defining the claimed design

The drawings section of the design patent application is the most important section because the drawings show what is and is not protected by the design patent (for an example of a design patent, see Appendix C).[10] That is, the drawings define the claimed design. The drawings should accurately represent what an inventor is seeking to protect. If the drawings do not match the look of the product, the issued design patent may not protect the product. For this reason, the design patent application should usually be filed as close to the product's launch date as possible so that the drawings can reflect any last-minute changes made to the product's design.

A design patent application appears simple to prepare, as it only requires drawings of different views of the product to show an ordinary observer what the product looks like. In general, a three-dimensional, perspective view is provided along with views of the front, back, top, left, right, and bottom (to see examples of these views, see Appendix C). These seven views are normally, but not always, sufficient to determine all the ornamentation to be protected by the design patent.

Additional views may also be necessary to fully illustrate the design. For example, a cross section view of the product may also be included to show blind crevices that would not be visible with the standard seven views.

The drawings may also convey the environment in which the product is used, but it should be made clear that this is not a part of the design being protected by the design patent. For example, the frame of a bicycle would constitute part of the environment for a patented rear suspension of a mountain bicycle. The environment is included to bring context to the part being protected by a design patent. To accurately reflect what is and is not protected by the design patent, the environment, and anything for which protections are not being sought, should be drawn in dash dot lines (i.e., phantom lines). The product and the ornamentation that the inventor wants protected should be drawn in solid dark lines. The design of the rear suspension should therefore be placed in solid lines and the frame of the bicycle along with all other components in phantom lines.

When deciding what to place in solid lines, it is helpful to understand the logic of determining the scope of protection that may be afforded in a design patent. The design patent will be composed of drawings of the patented design which define the scope of the design patent protection. It is difficult to understand which features should be placed in solid lines and which should not without understanding how to determine the scope of protection afforded under the design patent.

The more features placed in solid lines, the narrower the scope of patent protection. For example, if the product has three distinct features, all included in the design patent, a third-party could incorporate two of those features but make the third feature radically different and possibly avoid patent infringement. If the design patent protects only the primary feature (i.e., the main, ornamental feature of the product), and if this main ornamental feature were incorporated into the products sold by a third-party regardless of whether the third-party incorporates the other two features, the third-party's products would infringe on that design patent. In the latter case, because the design patent is broader in scope, it would be more difficult to avoid design patent infringement. If all three features are important, however, each may be protected by three different design patents, assuming each design feature is patentable.

Just as including multiple features in one design application can unduly narrow the scope of the patent's protection, so too can adding unnecessary details to any given feature in the application. When more details are added to the drawings, a third-party would have to incorporate all those features to infringe against the design patent. For example, in the case of *Arc'Teryx Equip, Inc. v. Westcomb Outerwear, Inc.,*[11]Arc'Teryx sued Westcomb for patent infringement on its patented jacket. Westcomb was selling a jacket aesthetically similar to Arc'Teryx's. However, the zipper on Westcomb's jacket did not come up the center and up under the chin but instead was offset to come up to the side of the chin. The District Court held that the defendant (Westcomb) did not infringe on the design shown in Arc'Teryx's design patent based on the visual differences between the zipper designs of the two jackets. The zipper in Arc'Teryx's design patent has two sections while the zipper of Westcomb's jacket has three sections (see Figure 5 below). Arc'Teryx (the patent owner) did not include variants of its offset zipper in its design patent. Westcomb (the defendant) was therefore able to utilize a design that looked different to avoid design patent infringement. In some cases, as in Arc'Teryx's, it is important to protect variations of a design for broader protection even if those variants are not being sold.

Arc' Teryx Design Patent   **Accused Infringer's Jacket**
(Westcomb Mirage Jacket)

Figure 5

To mitigate such easy design arounds, multiple versions (i.e., embodiments) of the same product can be incorporated into a single design patent application. The design patent application could then provide protection for alternative embodiments and variants of the product. In the case of the jacket above, the inventor could have included different configurations of the multi-section zipper and secured more patents on similar designs to make it more difficult to design around a portfolio of design patents. However, this technique may be expensive since additional drawing sheets and design patents incur extra fees, but it may be worth the expense.

Side Note: The patent examiner may render a "restriction requirement" against each design variant in a design patent application. A restriction requirement means that the examiner has determined that each of the embodiments should have been placed in a separate design patent application and the applicant must choose only one of the embodiments for examination in the current application and leave the others for examination in other divisional design patent applications, which can be filed at any time (see FAQ #10-16 in Section 3). These additional divisional design patent applications may, in some cases, be worth the additional cost (see FAQ #22-#29 in Section 3).

CHAPTER 9

Cost Considerations for Provisional and Nonprovisional Utility Patent Applications

A provisional patent application, when prepared properly, is less expensive than a nonprovisional patent application, but not by much. A well-prepared, provisional patent application is not a cheap option.

Similarities and differences between provisional and nonprovisional patent applications

To understand the difference in costs between provisional and nonprovisional patent applications, one needs to know the similarities and differences of both types of application in addition to the effort each requires. Those similarities and differences are discussed here and are listed in Table 3 below.

Both provisional and nonprovisional applications are similar in that they both establish a date of invention as well as provide patent pendency protection for the concepts, features, and information included in a nonprovisional patent application. Any information not included in the nonprovisional patent application is not patent pending.

The primary difference is that the provisional patent application will be abandoned by operation of law (i.e., automatically discarded) twelve months after its filing date unless a corresponding nonprovisional application is filed.

By contrast, a nonprovisional application automatically enters the queue for examination and is eventually assigned to an examiner to examine the application for patent. The nonprovisional patent application is only abandoned if the applicant fails to respond to an office action or explicitly abandons the patent application.

Provisional applications cost about twenty percent less than nonprovisional applications (when prepared properly)

Cost is a minor difference between provisional and nonprovisional patent applications. When prepared properly, the cost of a provisional patent application is about twenty percent less than the cost of a nonprovisional patent application. The price of a patent application includes fees for attorney time along with the costs associated with governmental filing and computer-generated drawings. Fees based on the time spent on the project by the attorney constitute most of the price for a patent application. The difference in cost of the two types of patent applications can therefore be best understood by enumerating the time devoted by an attorney to both.

A nonprovisional application includes the following sections:
1. The "Background," which describes the problem solved by the invention.
2. The "Brief Summary," which briefly describes the inventive solution to the problem described in the Background.
3. The "Brief Description of the Drawings," which describes the drawings included in the application.
4. The "Detailed Description," which should explain the full scope of the invention including the point of novelty, variations of important aspects, minimally viable product, sub-optimal competitive alternatives, and

other information necessary for properly describing the invention and understanding the claims. Eighty to ninety percent of an attorney's time preparing a nonprovisional application is spent on this section.

5. The "Claim Set," which defines the "metes and bounds" of the invention that the inventor is claiming as the invention.

6. The "Abstract," which briefly summarizes the Detailed Description.

7. The "Computer-Aided Drawings," or black line drawings, which associate the drawings with the text of the patent application with reference numerals.

The sections required for both nonprovisional and provisional patent applications are marked with an "X" below in Table 3.

	Nonprovisional Application	Provisional Application
Background	X	
Brief Summary	X	
Brief Description of the Drawings	X	
Detailed Description	X	X
Claims	X	
Abstract	X	
Drawings	X	X

Table 3

Patent attorneys spend *most* of their time on the *Detailed Description section* when preparing a nonprovisional application. In the Detailed Description section, the invention should be described in detail including how to make and use the invention as well as any desired variants, options, or the "minimally competitive alternative product."[12]The Detailed Description should be crafted carefully to not limit the scope of protection afforded by the patent's claims. The Detailed Description also forms the basis for the terms used in the claim language (see Chapter 10). Hence, *eighty to ninety percent* of my time preparing a nonprovisional application is spent on the Detailed Description.

As the above chart indicates, only the Drawings and the Detailed Description are required to prepare and file a provisional application (other sections may be included, but they are not required). Since the Detailed Description, which is required in both types of applications, makes up the bulk of the cost associated with a nonprovisional patent application, the provisional patent application is made less costly only by excluding sections that are not required. The Background, Brief Summary, Brief Description of the Drawings, Detailed Description, Claims, Abstract and Drawings sections, are not required, are *easy* to prepare, and do not require a significant amount of time (note: the claims section does take more time than the others).[13] I only spend about ten to twenty percent of my time on these other sections. Hence, the provisional patent application is not cheap and is only slightly less expensive due to fewer required sections.

Cheap provisional patent applications on the internet

The Internet contains a lot of information about provisional patent applications, falsely describing them as "the poor man's patent," "a low- cost patent," and "the cheap patent." This is a mischaracterization of the provisional patent application. It would be better characterized as a *lower-cost* alternative to the nonprovisional patent application, as described by the USPTO. A low-priced provisional application may be of poor quality and ineffective for providing the type of patent protection the inventor wants and/or needs.

Inventors can find a wide range of prices, as low as five hundred dollars, for provisional patent applications on the internet. Some of these prices cover only the filing of the provisional patent application and not its preparation. In this scenario, the inventor prepares the application and the patent agent or attorney verifies that the application forms are in order. The patent attorney does not normally review the actual substance of the patent application. At this cost a patent attorney may provide a minimal review of the Detailed Description, However, it most likely does not fully describe the invention or protect the inventor.

A well-prepared patent application should disclose the invention's point of novelty as well as other variants and options. For example, if part of the invention includes a screw fastener, the Detailed Description should likely include other types of fasteners including nails, latches, clips, etc. It should not describe only what the inventor invented, otherwise the description may be too narrow and the full scope of the invention may not be adequately protected by the patent.

Even though the cost of such a patent application found on the internet is less, a low cost provisional patent application could cost the inventor more money overall since a patent attorney may need to mitigate any negative impacts later on. For example, if the way that the patent application describes the invention causes the claims to be narrowly construed or interpreted, third-party competitors may easily design around the patent's claims. The inventor could not sue for damages and an injunction. If the patent application is not properly drafted to mitigate any narrowing interpretation of the claims, it may ultimately prove to be a waste of money.

Investment in a skilled patent attorney will save you time and money in the long run

An improperly prepared patent application may prohibit an inventor from securing effective protection for an invention. Although patent attorneys are fallible, the quality will be better than if inventors draft patent applications themselves.

I have reviewed many applications prepared by inventors and many are poorly written, do not address the proper points that need to be addressed, and fail to include essential information about the invention, such as the point of novelty. Often, if inventors choose to prepare a patent application without help, they reach out to a patent attorney only after encountering problems later. At that point, a patent attorney may require significant time to fix the issues. This will cost a significant amount of money to fix and meet the inventor's end goals (such as receiving broad patent protection to sufficiently protect the product), if it is even possible. Utilizing competent patent counsel from the very beginning mitigates these issues.

To be clear, I am not against using a provisional patent application to establish patent pendency. There are, in my opinion, strategies for utilizing the provisional patent application (see Chapter 4 and Chapter 7). If an inventor is going to expend the time and money to secure a patent or launch a business, the process of securing the patent should be done properly. Moreover, this process is not cheap despite claims found on the internet. If an inventor tries to cut corners, the costs of going through the patent process may be much higher than expected in the long run and not worthwhile. Hiring a competent patent attorney might require a higher, initial investment, but will likely save time and money with better results.

CHAPTER 10

Overarching Principles of a Utility Patent Application

The overarching principles below are a useful guide for understanding the written description, drawings, and claims in a utility patent application. These principles are difficult to internalize, implement, and apply without the mentoring of an experienced patent attorney, and I do not advocate that inventors or startups draft patent applications without competent patent counsel. Use this information to better interact with patent counsel.

Attorneys require years to learn the art of preparing a patent application. From this experience, patent attorneys learn to balance opposing goals. For example, the first goal is to secure broad claims to block competitors from competing with the inventor in the marketplace. A second, opposing goal is to present sufficiently narrow claims to avoid the prior art so that the USPTO will grant a patent on the invention. The following, overarching principles are a useful guide for trying to understand the various goals which may oppose each other in preparing a patent application for filing and prosecution before the USPTO.

Point of novelty

Identifying the point of novelty is crucial for drafting a patent application. See Chapter 1 for more information about the point of novelty. Inventors often dream up different uses of their inventions and worry about how others might be able to copy or design around their idea. They may eventually lose focus on the point of novelty over a period of time. Properly identifying the point of novelty and remaining focused on the point of novelty focuses everyone's efforts. For example, identifying the point of novelty will help determine what should be included in a patent application. Including minor aspects of the product that are unrelated to the point of novelty increases the time and expense spent drafting a patent application without any significant benefit. Inventors and their patent attorneys should take time to identify the point of novelty of the invention to clarify the important aspects of the invention that need to be covered in the patent application.[14]

The point of novelty also forms the basic outline of the patent application. The point of novelty should be repeatedly described in multiple sections of the patent application— Claims, Abstract, Brief Summary, and the Detailed Description—and should be, as far as possible, illustrated in the Drawings. Ultimately, the point of novelty should be prominent and clarified throughout the patent application. An attorney's goal when writing a patent application should be to make the point of novelty clear and up-front to the reader (i.e., inventor, investor, judge, jury, competitor).

During patent prosecution, the invention, as it is recited in the claims, is viewed as a whole. But when thinking through the drafting process of the patent application, it is helpful to prepare the draft patent application based on the point of novelty.

During examination, the examiner may provide prior art references that disclose the point of novelty. In this scenario, the focus of the claims should be shifted to an alternative embodiment, or a different aspect of the point of novelty. If the examiner cites a prior art reference that is close, but not identical, to the point of novelty, the claims may have to be narrowed. If, as in the example of the mechanical pencil in Chapter 1, the cited prior art disclosed a mechanical clicker mechanism, the claims may have to be narrowed to focus on a specific, unique feature of the mechanical clicker mechanism to distinguish it from the cited prior art reference and obtain the patent. Accordingly, a patent application should be drafted with the possibility of claiming a narrow aspect of the point of novelty or claiming a different point of novelty altogether in the future during the examination stage. After filing, the patent application cannot be altered by adding new matter or deleting information from the patent application. As such, whatever strategy one might want to employ during the examination stage, the information to implement that strategy must be included in the patent application at the time of filing.

In sum, articulating the point of novelty is essential to deciding what to include and exclude from a patent application. It is also important to structure the patent application so that the focus of the claims can be narrowed or shifted if, and when, needed during the examination stage.

Enablement requirement

The "enablement requirement" is stated in 35 U.S.C. § 112(a) and dictates that the patent application enable one of ordinary skill in the art to which the invention pertains to make and use the full scope of the claimed invention.[15] That is, the enablement requirement demands a kind of instruction set or "recipe" for the invention that describes the important relationships between the product's different structures in such a way that one of ordinary skill in the art can make and use the invention. In the mechanical pencil example, the relationship between the removable eraser and the body of the pencil may be important to its basic functioning. The user may need to remove the eraser from the pencil body to add additional lead rods. Additionally, the internal clicker mechanism needs to be explained in detail so that an engineer could understand how to design and produce it. An applicant must include a description of the product explaining how to "make" and "use" it in the Detailed Description section. This is like an instruction manual included with products when they are sold.

This requirement surprises some inventors who wish to keep the workings of their inventions secret. However, disclosure of the invention to the public is an inventor's part of the contract they have with the U.S. government. The government is willing to issue a patent granting exclusionary rights to an inventor for a limited period. This is the government's part of the contract. In exchange, inventors teach others how to make and use the invention. If inventors did not do so, the public (once the patent term has expired) would not benefit from those inventions. The enablement requirement ensures that the public will benefit from inventions after the granted patent expires.

Best mode requirement

The "best mode requirement" is also stated in 35 U.S.C. § 112(a) and requires the inventor to disclose the best way known by the inventor to implement the invention.[16] This does not require that the best mode, conceivable by anyone, be included in the patent application. It only requires that the best mode known by the inventor *at the time of filing* be included in the patent application. Also, if a better mode is conceived of *after* the filing of the patent application, it could not have been included in the patent. If the inventor designs a better mode of carrying out the invention after the filing of the patent application, the patent would still satisfy the best mode requirement and its validity would not be in jeopardy.

Sometimes, inventors want to exclude the best mode from the patent application in an attempt to protect it as a trade secret. However, fulfilling the best mode requirement is required by law to obtain a patent. Even though the examiner rarely rejects a patent application when the best mode requirement is not met, I nevertheless recommend doing so as it is in the best interest of the inventor.

If the best mode is not disclosed in the patent application, the inventor cannot seek protection for it. The best mode is presumably the preferred mode among many, and not including it in the application would force the inventor to pursue only a broad claim that would be more likely to be rejected. The inventor might not have the option of narrowing the claims to avoid the prior art for obtaining a patent. For example, if prior art is found that already teaches the broad, claimed concept, the examiner would reject the application and not issue a patent. If the best mode was included in the patent application, then the inventor has the option to narrow the claims to the best mode. If the best mode was not included, the contents of the patent application are fixed and unchangeable upon its filing and new information cannot be added to an application after the filing date. In this case, the invention would have no option for narrowing the claims to get around the cited prior art. The best mode should therefore be included in the original patent application so that the claims can be narrowed to the best mode in this situation.

Best mode requirement issues frequently arise with chemical or drug formulations. Inventors may want to keep the specific ingredients of a formulation secret while seeking to protect the generic formulation. This is not advised because, in addition to the above reasons, the inventor and patent attorney have a duty of good faith and candor to the USPTO. Failure to disclose the best mode may be considered a breach of this duty and have serious implications during enforcement of the patent.

Written description requirement

The patent application must satisfy the written description requirement[17] by disclosing the invention in the textual description and drawings of the patent application. To meet this requirement, the patent specification (i.e., the actual text and drawings found in the patent application) must show that the inventor conceived of (i.e., possessed) the claimed invention. Otherwise, the claims will be deemed invalid for failing to satisfy the written description requirement.

For example, in *Gentry Gallery, Inc. v. Berkline Corp.*, Gentry (the patent owner) sued Berkline (the accused infringer) for patent infringement on its patented sectional sofa with a control center. At issue was whether the sofa, which the inventor claimed to possess, included a control center (i.e., storage for a remote control) at *any* location on the sofa. The Claims section stated that the invention was a sectional sofa that included a control center. The patent specification, however, described the control center in a *specific* location but did not appear to suggest other possible locations for the control center. The court interpreted the absence of alternative locations for the control center in the patent as demonstrating that the inventor did not conceive of (i.e., possess) a sofa with a control center placed at *any* location. The court maintained therefore that the patent did not satisfy the written description requirement because it did not show that the inventor possessed the claimed invention of a sofa with a console that could be located anywhere. Even though the Claims section did not *limit* the location of the console to one area, the patent's specification made clear that the invention conceived of only a version with the control center at one particular location. To avoid this interpretation, the patent drafter should have described the control console's location as a preferred location and then included descriptions of other possible locations.

The written description requirement also necessitates that the specification provide support or antecedent basis for each example of the claim terms and phrases found in the Claims section. That is, the other sections of the patent application must reference and explain if needed the terms used in the Claim section. For example, claim 1, shown in column 6 of the patent example in Appendix B, refers to "an upper link pivotably attached to the front frame." The term "upper link" is identified as reference numeral 40 and "front frame" as reference numeral 12 in columns 3 and 4 of the patent example in Appendix B. These parts are discussed in the patent's Detailed Description in column 3, line 12, column 4, and line 13 as well as shown in Figures 1 and 2. Because of this explanation in the patent's Detailed Description, someone reading the claims could understand the meaning of the phrase "an upper link pivotably attached to the front frame" as it is used in the claims of the Claim Section. The specification in this instance provides antecedent *basis* for the claim language.

The Manual of Patent Examining Procedure (MPEP) states that the patent specification should ideally serve as a glossary for terms found in the Claims Section of the patent application. This is so the examiner and the public can clearly ascertain the meaning of the claim terms. The rules (37 CFR 1.75(d)(1)) require that the claim terms find clear support or antecedent basis in the specification so that the meaning of the claim terms may be ascertainable by reference to the specification. Following this rule also helps to satisfy the statutory written description requirement.

Simply put, the patent application is a written explanation (i.e., text and drawings) of the invention that should cover the point of novelty and details thereof. An inventor should not rely on features and aspects that could be merely implied by the text and drawings. It may seem a simple suggestion to make explicit that which is implicit in the text and drawings, but it is actually very difficult to do. Patent attorneys work on this when drafting a patent application. The inventor must also review and check that this has been done. This will increase the likelihood that all patent requirements are met and minimize potential, future litigation issues.

The case of *Crown Packaging v. Ball Metal*[18] illustrates the difficulty of making explicit that which might be implicit in the text of the patent application. Crown Packaging (the patent owner) sued Ball Metal (the accused infringer) for patent infringement on its soda can, which was made with less aluminum than the prior art. In the patent application, the inventor described two different areas of the can that could be modified to reduce the amount of aluminum used: the chuck wall (Figure 6, #24, below) and the reinforcing bead (Figure 6, #25, below). However, the specification of the patent only included an explanation for two different areas in *conjunction* with, not independent from, each other. The contended issue was whether the application implicitly taught that only one area of the can, versus both areas simultaneously, required modification.[19]

This case illustrates that reasonable minds can have different interpretations of a patent application's implicit content. The District Court and the Federal Circuit arrived at different conclusions as to what was implicitly taught by the patent. Although difficult, the goal of drafting a patent application is to make explicit those important aspects that might be implicit within the text of the patent application. Inventors ought to review the patent application carefully and provide feedback to the patent attorney to be sure that all the inventor's ideas are explicitly stated and not omitted or left implicit.

When there is a combination of aspects (e.g., chuck wall and reinforcing bead) that work in conjunction with each other to achieve a goal (e.g., reduce aluminum usage), it may be useful to state explicitly within the specification that the inventor contemplates that each aspect may achieve the goal either in combination with each other or individually. This is just one example of how one can make implicit features explicit. There are many more blind spots that writers have that prevent one from making explicit that which is implied by the text.

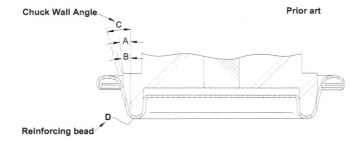

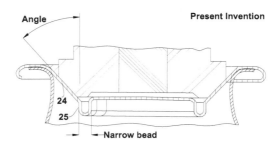

Figure 6

In another comparable example, *Revolution Eyewear, Inc. v. Aspex Eyewear,*[20] Aspex Eyewear (patent owner) contended that Revolution (accused infringer) infringed on its patented, removable sunglass lenses.[21] The patent described sunglass lenses that attach to the prescription lenses with magnets. In the prior art, sunglass lenses were attached by mounting magnets in the frame of the prescription glasses rather than on the lenses. But this setup weakened the frame, which caused the sunglass lenses to fall off. Aspex Eyewear's patented invention solved this problem by magnetically mounting the sunglass lenses directly onto projections built on the prescription lenses.[22]

The defendant (Revolution) attempted to avoid liability by asserting that the invention failed to meet the written description requirement since the claims described the solution to only one of the problems and not both (i.e., decreased strength and stable support). Hence, Revolution argued, Aspex's patent did not show the inventor had possession or conception of an invention that solved both problems, and Aspex had not satisfied the written description requirement and their patent should be invalidated. The court disagreed with Revolution. The court held that inventors can craft claims to address one or several problems and that the written description requirement is satisfied for each claim as long as the description conveys that the inventor was in possession of the invention recited in the claims.

Although Aspex (patent owner) survived the challenge to its patent, this case illustrates the dangers of preparing one's own patent by a lay person. It illustrates the types of arguments that accused infringers and defendants may raise to avoid patent infringement liability. A patent application prepared without legal counsel is more susceptible to this type of attack since lay people would not be *aware* of these types of issues.

Moreover, the *Aspex* case illustrates that the benefits of an invention should be explained separately and not as if they are interdependent (i.e., described as disjunctive instead of conjunctive). For example, the benefits of a mechanical pencil may be that it does not require a sharpener and can consistently produce lines of uniform width. To write a disjunctive description, the patent application may highlight the various aspects of the mechanical pencil that can be configured to achieve either one or both benefits (i.e., these benefits should be described not as dependent upon each other, but achievable independent of each other).

This written description requirement, among others, might be discussed in a DIY patent drafting handbook. However, a layperson would have difficulty drafting a proper written description. A patent attorney learns how to write a well-crafted description of the invention through years of practice and mentoring by a senior patent attorney. The patent application should describe the invention in sufficient detail so that it is clear that the inventor had possession or conceived of the claimed invention. If the claims are too broad, the patent may be invalid for failing to satisfy the written description requirement. Without the aid of a patent attorney, a patent application's mistakes and weaknesses are usually uncovered only after filing, when the application is being examined, or after the application has matured into a patent and potential infringers have attempted to invalidate the patent. The mistakes sometimes cannot be resolved at that time.

The information in this section is meant to help you work more efficiently and thoughtfully with a patent attorney to create a better prepared patent application.

CHAPTER 11

Parts of a Utility Patent Application

Each patent application is a customized document that is designed to pitch the invention to investors, examiners, judges, and a jury. A few structural aspects and mechanical drafting techniques of a patent application are discussed in this section.

This chapter describes the purpose of each section of a provisional and nonprovisional utility patent application. As Table 4 below shows, there are seven different sections of a nonprovisional patent application, only two of which are required for a provisional application:

	Nonprovisional Application	Provisional Application
Background	X	
Brief Summary	X	
Brief Description of the Drawings	X	
Detailed Description	X	X
Claims	X	
Abstract	X	
Drawings	X	X

Table 4

The Detailed Description and Drawing sections are the minimum requirements to file and secure a filing date as a provisional application. One or more of the remaining sections *can* be included when filing an application as a provisional patent application. The Detailed Description, Drawings, and at least one claim in the Claims section are the minimum requirements to secure a filing date or patent pendency when filing a nonprovisional application. However, all seven sections are required to move forward into the examination stage with a nonprovisional patent application and to eventually secure a patent. If a patent application does not have all the required sections or does not follow the recommended arrangement, it will not satisfy the formal requirements of the USPTO. In that case, the USPTO will issue a notice of missing parts and the applicant will have time to provide the missing sections and rearrange the patent application. Please be aware that initially cutting corners may ultimately be costlier compared to properly preparing the patent application in the first place. It is best to invest the time and money to prepare the application correctly the first time.

Background section

The Background section of a utility patent application describes the current state of the prior art pertaining to the proposed invention and should not mention the present invention. An acceptable approach to writing the Background section is to be very brief and not disclose more than is required. Even though the USPTO recommends that the background section be filled with a good amount of information about the current state of the art, this is not the approach that I take. Should litigation occur, anything in the background section can, and will, be used to narrow the interpretation of the patent claims and avoid patent infringement liability.[23]

For example, in the case of the mechanical pencil invention, the Background section may be written as:

Paragraph 1: The various embodiments and aspects described herein relate to a writing instrument.

Paragraph 2: Various issues relating to writing instruments are known in the art. Accordingly, there is a need in the art for an improved writing instrument.

As the example above illustrates, the first paragraph of the Background section should be one sentence that sets the stage (i.e., field of the invention) for the present invention. A typical first paragraph of the Background section may use the phrasing: "The embodiments and aspects described herein relate to a [insert generic term for inventive product or process]." The second paragraph should briefly describe the state of the current prior art related to the invention and perhaps the problems or issues associated with the current technology such as cost or ease of use.

The case *Leo Pharmaceutical Products LTD v. PTO*[24] illustrates why the Background section should not provide an exhaustive explanation of the prior art. The *Leo* case involved a drug (vitamin D and corticosteroids) that an inventor had newly redesigned to be storage stable. Galderma (accused infringer) attempted to attack the validity of Leo Pharmaceutical Product's patent via an *inter partes* reexamination proceeding held at the USPTO.[25] Galderma contended that the claimed invention was an obvious combination of prior art references. The prior art disclosed compositions containing both vitamin D and corticosteroids. To obtain a storage stable composition, the inventor added a particular solvent to increase the stability of vitamin D and corticosteroids.

To defend against the invalidity attack, Leo (patent owner) contended that the prior art references did not recognize the need to combine the teachings of the two references to combine vitamin D and corticosteroids.[26] If the Background section *had* indicated the problem with the prior art, it could have been argued that it provides the necessary motivation to combine references to come up with the claimed invention and thus be an obvious variant of the prior art. However, if a patent owner does not highlight the problem in the Background section, the obviousness argument, or the invalidity argument to combine references that the accused infringer put forth, would not be available to invalidate the patent. In the case example above, Leo did not include problems with the prior art in the Background section. In the opinion, this absence was highlighted as a reason for non-obviousness. Thus, the patent owner successfully argued against this argument and won the *inter partes* reexamination.

The Background section is supposed to describe the current state of the art but is sometimes written in a way that also recognizes problems and potential solutions brought up by others in the field that might be used against the patent application or patent to show the invention as being obvious. If the specific problem had been recognized in the Background section in the above example, the solution (i.e., Leo's invention) may have been interpreted as an obvious variant of what was already known in the art. Identification of the problem in the Background section is sometimes used to show that the invention was not novel or obvious and thus not patentable. This case illustrates the advantage of omitting any information about the problem that led to the invention.

One should also avoid disparaging various techniques and features in the Background section, lest it be argued during litigation that the scope of patent protection does not encompass the disparaged techniques or features. To avoid patent infringement liability, competitors may design around the issued patent by incorporating a technique or feature that the patent owner disparaged in their own patent application. For example, in *Ultimate Pointer LLC v. Nintendo Co. Ltd.*,[27] Ultimate Pointer repeatedly disparaged indirect pointing devices in its patent application. The court construed the claim phrase "handheld device" (i.e., handheld pointing device), which appears broad enough to include both direct and indirect handheld pointing devices, to exclude indirect pointing devices because Ultimate Pointer had disparaged those types of devices. The logic of the court's conclusion is that Ultimate Pointer would not disparage a device that it wanted to protect. Ultimate Pointer lost the case and Nintendo avoided patent infringement liability by incorporating an indirect pointing device in its product.[28]

Side Note: If an inventor wants to submit a description of the current state of the prior art for the benefit of the examiner's knowledge, there are less risky options. For example, as discussed in Chapter 7, the inventor could submit an Information Disclosure Statement (IDS), which includes various, third-party, printed publications that disclose prior art information, or an article identifying the problems and issues related to the present invention. This information can also be presented to the examiner in the remarks section of a response to an Office Action or telephonic interview with the examiner. Presented this way, the negative impact of disclosing the information may be mitigated because it would be considered attorney arguments and information submitted *without a declaration* by the inventor. By contrast, if prior art problems are included in the patent application's Background section, it is submitted *with a declaration* wherein the inventor states, under penalty of perjury, the following statement: "I hereby state that I've reviewed and understood the contents of the above identified application, including the claims, as amended by any amendment specifically referred to above." Statements and comments made in the patent application may therefore be given more weight than statements made by an attorney. To mitigate detrimental effects, an applicant can include a *just* short, generic description of the prior art in the Background section and then supplement information about the prior art in an IDS, the remarks section of an Office Action, or a telephonic interview with the examiner.

Brief Summary section

The Brief Summary section summarizes the Detailed Description section and is typically written after the Detailed Description section has been drafted. This way, the drafter has the advantage of thinking through the invention while writing the Detailed Description section and can better summarize the invention in the Brief Summary section later.

The first paragraph should summarize the invention's point of novelty and benefit. The examiner is given a fixed amount of time to read and learn about the intricacies of the invention. The examiner can quickly identify the point of novelty of the invention if the applicant includes the point of novelty and that which the inventor wants to protect in the first paragraph. The subsequent paragraphs should further illustrate the various embodiments, features, and benefits of the present invention. However, in my opinion, it is better to use these paragraphs to restate the language found in the Claims section. This will help satisfy the patent rule that each term in the patent Claims section finds antecedent basis[29] within the patent specification, as discussed previously. Each term or phrase used in the Claims section should therefore be repeated in the Brief Summary section. The claims can be cut and pasted in the Brief Summary section after the first paragraph and then modified into sentence format.

Brief Description of the Drawings section

The Brief Description of the Drawings section provides a broad overview of the views shown in the Drawings section. Drawings should, according to patent rule, illustrate each feature in the claims. This section should be brief and does not need to be creative, attempt to indicate the point of novelty of the present invention, or describe its benefit. This section should merely indicate the various views of the drawings (e.g., perspective, left, right, top, bottom, front, and rear view) and whether the drawings are cross-sectioned. It may also identify the parts of the invention within each of the figures. For example, a description of the drawings for a mechanical pencil might read:

Figure 1 is a perspective view of a mechanical pencil;

Figure 2 illustrates lead as it is advanced out of the mechanical system body shown in Figure 1 as a mechanical clicker is being depressed;

Figure 3 is a cross sectional view of the mechanical clicker shown in Figure 2 before being depressed; and

Figure 4 is a cross sectional view of the mechanical clicker shown in Figure 2 after being depressed and the lead is advanced.

Detailed Description section

I spend eighty to ninety percent of my time on the Detailed Description when I prepare a nonprovisional patent application for a client. It should underscore the point of novelty, typically in the first paragraph. The examiner should be able to quickly identify the point of novelty in both the first paragraph of the Brief Summary and the Detailed Description section. Note, however, that the language describing the point of novelty in the first paragraph of the

Detailed Description section should be different than that used in the first paragraph of the Brief Summary section.

Subsequent paragraphs of the Detailed Description section should describe the various, alternative embodiments and features of the invention as well as contain reference numerals that refer to the figures in the Drawings section. One should be able to read the Detailed Description section and refer to the drawings for clarification. For an explanation of the numbering system, please see the section on the Drawings section below.

The description of the invention in the Brief Summary and Detailed Description section act as a dictionary for the terms and phrases used in the Claims section. It is therefore important to describe the invention clearly and concisely without unduly limiting the scope of the claim language and the scope of patent protection afforded by the claims of the patent.

The following discussions from this book should be reviewed to understand what should be included in the Detailed Description section:

- Chapter 1, Writing Tip #6 in Chapter 12 and Detailed Description section in Chapter 11 offer an extensive discussion on the point of novelty, minimally viable product, and how the specification within the Detailed Description acts as a sort of dictionary for the terms and phrases used in the Claims Section. It covers the overarching principles of the utility patent application and discusses the point of novelty, enablement requirement, best mode requirement, and the written description requirement.

- Chapter 12 covers eight writing tips on drafting the patent application. There is an extensive discussion on the preferred embodiments and sub-optimal embodiments in the Detailed Description along with other important topics.

Claims section

The claims in the Claim Set is the primary focus of the patent application because the claims define the scope of patent protection afforded by the patent. There must be at least one independent claim in a nonprovisional patent application. The claims should focus on the point of novelty and use terms and phrases to describe the invention's structure and/or method steps. The preparation and examination of the patent application begins and ends with the claims of the Claim Set, which defines the scope (i.e., metes and bounds) of protection afforded by the patent. The claims should therefore be broad enough to encompass competitive alternatives of the potential invention and to therefore hinder third parties from producing a similar product with which they could compete for the same customers. Narrow claims may pass through examination easier, but are generally less useful because a competitor would be able to easily design around the narrow claim and compete in the marketplace. They are useful in limited circumstances.

The Claims section is the most difficult to prepare properly. It should therefore be prepared by a competent patent attorney, not a layperson. A single word in a patent claim can unduly limit the scope of the protection afforded by the patent, narrowing its protection and enabling competitors to design around the invention and avoid infringement liability. What follows is not a tutorial on how to write a proper claim, only an introduction to claims of the Claims section so that a new inventor or layperson can rudimentarily understand how the claims work.[30]

The anatomy of a claim

The "Claim Set" is normally included at the back of the patent application or patent and starts with the phrase "what is claimed is," "I claim," or "we claim." Claims come in two varieties: an apparatus claim or a method claim. An apparatus claim is directed to a product. The method claim is a series of steps directed to the use of the product or some other steps in relation to the invention such as how the product is manufactured. The basic filing fee for a utility, nonprovisional application allows the inventor to present three independent claims (independent versus dependent claims, explained below), and a total of twenty claims (independent and dependent) at no additional cost. Each additional claim incurs a cost. Since cost is an issue for most inventors, the best approach is to present only high value claims within the "3–20 rule" above.[31]

An individual claim consists of three parts: preamble, transitional phrase, and claim limitations. Below is an example of a claim for the mechanical pencil invention:

A mechanical pencil for handwriting on a piece of paper, the pencil comprising:

>   a tubular body having a bottom and top ends;

>   a mechanical clicker system disposed on the tubular body; and

>   a removable eraser to access a depository for lead rods within the tubular body.

The preamble is first and usually starts with a phrase such as "an apparatus for [fill in the purpose of the apparatus]." In the example above it states: "A mechanical pencil for handwriting on a piece of paper." This is another way to say the same thing. The second part, the transitional phrase, is indicated by phrases such as "comprising," "consisting of" or "consisting essentially of." The example above states: "the pencil comprising." Each transitional phrase has a significantly different meaning and affects the scope of the patent differently. For the layperson, the most common transitional phrase is "comprising" since this is the broadest form of transitional phrase. Think of "comprising" as meaning "including, but not limited to." The third part is the body of the claim, and it lists the elements of the invention and the claim's limitations (this will be explained in more detail below).

Claims are either independent or dependent. A claim is independent if it does not depend on another claim, while claims that do depend on previous claims are referred to as dependent claims. The claims are sequentially numbered in this section. Claim 1 is normally an independent claim and does not refer to a different claim. Claim 2 is normally a dependent claim referring to Claim 1 and incorporates within itself all the limitations recited in Claim 1.

The above example would be considered an independent claim, which I will refer to as "Claim 1".

A claim dependent on Claim 1, labeled "Claim 2," might read:

2. The pencil of Claim 1 wherein the mechanical clicker system is positioned on the body adjacent to an index finger to allow the user to conveniently depress a button of the mechanical clicker system while using the pencil to write on the piece of paper.

By definition, Claim 1 is broader than Claim 2. Claim 2 is narrower than Claim 1 as it requires that the mechanical clicker system be located near the index finger position on the tubular body. A patent's broadest scope of protection is determined by the independent, not dependent, claims because it has less requirements that must be met in order to find that a product or method infringes. How to determine whether infringement exists is discussed below.

Since dependent claims do not determine the broadest scope of protection, one might ask why they are necessary. There are a variety of reasons for including dependent claims in the patent application. During the examination stage, the examiner uses prior art references to contend that the invention, as defined by the independent claims, is not novel. The examiner could assert that the claim is broad enough to encompass, or constitute an obvious variant of existing technology (i.e., the prior art anticipates the invention and therefore the invention is not novel). The dependent claims mitigate this potential issue by narrowing the broader, independent claims. The examiner may allow some of the narrower, dependent claims but not the broader, independent claims. In this case, the applicant only needs to amend the independent claims to incorporate the limitations of the allowed dependent claims to secure a patent.

In another situation, should litigation occur in which an accused infringer attempts to avoid patent infringement liability by attacking the novelty of independent claims,[32] and if independent claims are determined to be invalid, dependent claims may still be valid. If they are still valid, the dependent claims are used to determine whether the accused infringer is liable. As such, the dependent claims also help to increase the likelihood that a claim is still valid, albeit dependent, should an independent claim be invalidated during litigation.

The purpose of a claim: to determine the scope of patent protection

The claims of an issued patent, ideally, describe the invention's point of novelty and prohibit competitors from copying an invention's point of novelty lest they be liable for patent infringement. The claims should be sufficiently broad so that the competitor has to make one or more significant changes to its product so that the product would be placed at a disadvantage when competing in the market. If the claims focus on peripheral aspects of the product instead of the point of novelty, competitors may not have a significant barrier to entry and could easily design around the claim by not including that peripheral aspect into their product. It is therefore important to focus on the point of novelty in the Claims section rather than unrelated, minor improvements at least in the independent claims.

The scope of a claim is determined by limitations recited within the body of the claim. For example, a claim to a wooden pencil may recite:

1. An apparatus for making marks on a sheet of paper, the apparatus comprising (i.e., is made up of):

    A. an external protective member having a length longer than a width of the external protective member;

    B. a lead material disposed within the external protective member and held in place by the external protective member; and

    C. an eraser attached to an upper portion of the external protective member.

The wooden pencil claim includes three elements: (A) external protective member, (B) lead material, and (C) eraser. A competitor must incorporate all three elements to infringe on the wooden pencil claim. Table 5 below illustrates how to determine if a device literally infringes on the pencil claim above. The first column refers to the three elements listed above. Product numbers 1-5 refer to hypothetical versions of the product that a competitor might create. These hypothetical products may incorporate some of the pencil's elements, or a new element, "D."

Claim Elements	Product 1	Product 2	Product 3	Product 4	Product 5
A	X	X		X	X
B	X	X	X		X
C	X		X	X	X
			D		D

Table 5

If a competitor incorporates elements A and B only (i.e., product 2), he or she is not infringing on the wooden pencil claim because the competitor did not incorporate element C and therefore did not include all three of the pencil's defining elements. The same is true for Products 3 and 4. Product 1, however, is literally infringing on the pencil claim because it incorporates all three of the pencil's claim elements. If a competitor incorporates an element "D" in addition to all three elements A, B, and C (product 5), the competitor still infringes on the wooden pencil claim. The addition of element D does not negate that the infringer incorporated elements A, B, and C into its pencil. Product 5 therefore literally infringes on the pencil claim.

In the above claim, each paragraph contains one element. This is a simplified approach to thinking about claim scope and infringement. However, each word of a claim may be a limitation that must be incorporated into the competitive product for it to be liable for infringement. Any change to the competitive product that does not incorporate all the elements as described by the claim may enable the competitor to avoid infringement. For example, in our wooden pencil example, the eraser is described as being at the top of the external protective member. If a competitor made a pencil without an eraser, that product would not literally infringe on the wooden pencil claim.

A product is analyzed to see if it incorporates all the limitations of a patented invention's claims to determine whether it literally infringes on a claim of the patent. If a court determines that the competitor's product does incorporate all the elements of the claims, the product literally infringes on the claims of the patented invention.

Even if a product does not literally infringe a claim, the defendant may still be liable for infringement under the Doctrine of Equivalents which broadens the scope of the claims beyond its literal scope.

Generating the Claim Set

Most inventors believe that securing the broadest patent protection *from the start* is the best strategy. Broad patent protection may be possible, but is often expensive. Broader claims are more likely to be rejected and the rejection maintained during the examination process for being anticipated by the prior art and/or considered obvious. An inventor could argue with the examiner and fight for the broadest claim scope desired and then *slowly* narrow the claim, but that strategy would expend considerable resources. A strategy that I have implemented for many solo inventors and startups is to initially seek a medium-scope claim, one which provides a significant barrier to entry for competitors but is hopefully easier to obtain. I do not recommend a strategy that initially seeks to secure a patent with a narrow scope without a specific reason. For some inventors, mere ownership of a patent, even with a narrow scope, may be valuable. However, inventors should understand the severe limitations provided by such a patent and such a strategy should not be implemented unless the inventor has a clear understanding of its limitations.

The basic process of generating a Claim Set involves thinking about all the potential entities that might want to infringe on the claimed invention. This may include all the entities along the chain of distribution including, but not limited to, the manufacturer, distributor, retailer, and end user. Inventors should consider including claims that address each of these in a patent application when submitting the patent application for examination. For example, a claim regarding the method for making a mechanical pencil may be ideal to get a manufacturer to be liable for patent infringement, but it would not permit the patent owner to sue an end user who only uses, but does not manufacture, the mechanical pencil. Likewise, a claim directed to the method for using the mechanical pencil may be ideal to get an end user to be liable for patent infringement, but not permit the patent owner to sue a manufacturer. The method for making the mechanical pencil is likely more valuable than its method of use because the inventor would presumably want to stop the manufacturer rather than the end user (since it may not be economically feasible to sue all individual end users).[33]

The default rule for listing claims in the patent application is to present the broadest claim as Claim 1.[34] Each successive dependent claim narrows the scope of protection of Claim 1. Each successive independent claim should address a different entity (such as the manufacturer or end user) or focus on a different aspect of the invention or point of novelty in an attempt to provide broad coverage collectively with all of the independent claims. For example, if independent Claim 1 is directed to the apparatus, the second independent claim could address the method of manufacture. The inclusion of a claim addressing the method of manufacture can preclude another manufacturer from making and selling the product against the will of the patent owner. The third independent claim could focus on a different entity along the chain of distribution.[35]

An examiner may allow some, but not all, claims. If the allowable claims have a medium breadth, canceling the rejected claims and letting the allowable claims to mature into a patent may be the best course of action. The broader, rejected claims can be sought in a subsequent application that claims priority back to the first, parent, patent application.[36]

In particular, the scope of patent protection can be broadened by filing a "continuation patent application." The continuation patent application can be filed, and claim priority back to the first, parent application, any time before the parent patent issues or is abandoned. Clients sometimes ask whether the filing of the continuation patent application will delay the patent grant based on the parent application. The answer is no. If the parent application has allowed claims, and the inventor has decided to pay the issue fee so that a patent is granted on the allowed claims, the filing of the continuation patent application does not affect the timing of the grant of the parent patent. The continuation patent application is a refiling of the parent application with a Claim Set that can mimic the allowed claims but be slightly broader so as to improve the scope of patent protection for the invention. For more information about filing a continuation patent, (see FAQ #22-#29 in Section 3).

Abstract section

The Abstract section is a short summary (no more than 150 words) about the point of novelty and may be shorter than the first paragraphs of the Brief Summary and the Detailed Description section. The Abstract is typically drafted after writing the first paragraphs of the Detailed Description and Brief Summary so that the drafter has the benefit of thinking through the invention's point of novelty before drafting the Abstract section. If the Abstract section contains more than 150 words, it is not fatal to the patent application, but the examiner will object to it and require the applicant to amend the abstract to comply with the 150- word limit.

Drawing set

A reader will often immediately skim through the drawings to get a feel for what is being disclosed in an application or patent. In a utility patent application, the drawings provide a basic outline of the *functional or utilitarian* features of the invention. In contrast, the drawings for a design patent show what *ornamental* design is protected. The drawings set the stage for the reviewer and provide insight into what the reader can expect when reviewing the text. The drawings are therefore reviewed more often than the text of the patent specification. For this reason, drawings may be more important than the text in this way. As such, the drawings section deserves much attention during the preparation process. Section 608.02 of the Manual of Patent Examining Procedure provides details for satisfying the drawing requirements when preparing a patent application.[37]

Drawings may be hand-sketched in a provisional patent application but must be depicted in clear black solid lines in a nonprovisional application. They are typically computer drawn. The various figures in the drawing section should tell a story such that a reader can have a basic understanding of what the point of novelty might be. I highly recommend utilizing a professional patent draftsperson[38] after first creating an initial, basic flow of the drawings. In the mechanical pencil example, the first figure could present the mechanical pencil in hand with the index finger on the mechanical clicker system. The second and third figures could present cross sectional views of the mechanical clicker system showing the button in a non-depressed and depressed state to illustrate how the lead rod advances through the mechanical clicker system. The last figure could show the removal of an eraser to demonstrate access of the lead rod to a depository within the tubular body. The figures show a story of how the mechanical pencil is used and thereby illustrate the point of novelty.

Side Note: In the text, reference numbers are linked to corresponding reference numbers in the drawings. Reference numerals normally start with "10" and are sequentially incremented by two. If, upon review of the patent application, more numbers are necessary, odd numbers may be used to maintain sequential order in the text. No single reference number may be used to refer to different parts.

General Patent Application Writing Tips

This chapter describes some of the (sometimes counterintuitive) guidelines and good practice tips for drafting a patent application.

Below are general guidelines and approaches I have developed for preparing a patent application. These are not fixed rules—most have exceptions—nor are they designed to teach how to draft a patent application. They simply reflect my personal approach. Also included are answers to clients' frequently asked questions after having reviewed a patent application that I have drafted for them.

Writing Tip #1:
How to write an application with the broadest possible protection (without breaking the bank)

All my clients express a desire to get the most effective, broadest scope patent protection for their inventions. During consultations, a few inventors describe the invention in terms of overall goals and how the mechanisms of the invention can achieve them without describing how the invention actually works. They do this because they believe if they describe their invention generically, they can influence me to write a broad application and secure a broad patent. However, a broad patent does not describe an invention in generic terms without any details. To secure a broad patent, the claims should be drafted in generic terms, but the Detailed Description should include as many details related to the point of novelty as possible. The more detail that is included into the Detailed Description of the patent application, the better.

Why include details and specifics of the invention in the Detailed Description section of the application if the claims are what define the scope of the patent protection? An important reason to include the particulars of the invention is that by law, the Detailed Description section must provide a written description that support the full scope of the claim(s). Otherwise, a patent may be invalidated for failing to satisfy the written description requirement (see Chapter 10).

Furthermore, the inventor might not be able to secure patent protection for a generic version of the invention. The claims might be so broad that they encompass prior art devices. Information in the Detailed Description can be used to amend and narrow the rejected claims just enough to avoid the prior art (i.e., make them more specific and a little less broad so that they don't encompass the prior art). Without the details of the invention included in the Detailed Description section at the time of filing, the claims cannot be amended since no new information can be added to the patent application after it is filed with the USPTO. Therefore, the slightly narrower invention that might have been allowed, if it had not been included, cannot then be claimed. The inventor could not therefore avoid the prior art by including more detail in the claim or shifting its focus because that detail would not be in the patent application and the claim could not be amended and would remain rejected.

The Detailed Description should include alternative embodiments, peripheral aspects related to the point of novelty, and different "genus- species" combinations. The Claim Set, by contrast, should include only the invention's necessary components while the claims recite only the necessary elements directed to the point of novelty. This sets up the patent application to seek broad patent protection and allows the claims to be narrowed in the future during examination if necessary to secure the patent during examination.

Should the examiner find a prior art reference, which is directly on point to the broad concept of the invention, the inventor would have options for securing patent protection even if the protection is narrower than the inventor had initially hoped for.

This issue is illustrated in the case of *Bimeda R & D Limited*[39] in which a drug formulation inventor appealed the examiner's final rejection to the Federal Circuit. According to the application claims, the drug formulation excluded acriflavine, a type of antibiotic. Acriflavine was disclosed in the prior art reference cited by the examiner to reject the claims. To overcome the rejection, the inventor excluded it from the claims and argued the amended claims were patentable. Unfortunately for the inventor, the Detailed Description section of the patent only described a drug formulation that did not include antibiotics *in general* and the patent application did not exclude Acriflavine in particular. The Federal Court therefore held that the patent application did not support a claim specifically directed to an acriflavine-free formulation, and the inventor's claim to the acriflavine-free formulation was not allowable for not being supported by the original specification. If *Bimeda R & D Limited* had included a description that the drug formulation was free of a specific type of antibiotic such as acriflavine in the patent application, the inventor could have sought a claim to the drug formulation that is free of that specific type of antibiotic. But the inventor did not do so and the claim was held invalid.

When drafting a patent application, include the particulars of the invention in the Detailed Description section. If it is necessary to rely on those details, the claims can be amended during examination to include those details in the independent or dependent claims, and the patent application may be salvaged.

Writing Tip #2:
Be explicit. Don't rely on inferences made in the patent application

When drafting the patent application, be explicit about the mechanics of your invention. Do not assume anyone will infer the same information you believe is implied in the text. For example, if a mechanical pencil has a high degree of rigidity (e.g., it is made from a hard form of plastic versus a softer type of plastic), which helps with its mechanical operation, the rigidity needs to be expressed in mechanical terms in the patent application. Do not rely on the examiner to infer from a description of the pencil's operation that the mechanical pencil *requires* a certain degree of rigidity— make it explicit.

Focusing on the point of novelty can help the patent drafter explicitly describe the various aspects of the invention. The drafter should focus on as many aspects of the point of novelty as possible and build the application around it. For example, if it is the mechanism that automatically progresses lead through a mechanical pencil makes the pencil novel, all aspects of that mechanism should be described in the Detailed Description. First, describe the basic operation of the mechanism. Second, include various parts of the mechanism that might help with, or improve, the functioning of the mechanism. If there are two or more such aspects that improve the function of the mechanism, such as (1) an index finger operated mechanical clicker and

(2) a thumb operated mechanical clicker it may be prudent to indicate that the inventive product may be fabricated by incorporating aspect number one only, aspect number two only, or combinations thereof (see Chapter 10, "Written Description Requirement," for more detail on describing features in a disjunctive manner).

Being explicit in the Detailed Description section is also important if patent protection is sought in foreign countries. Claims are often amended during examination of the patent application to avoid the prior art. In the United States, the USPTO has a more liberal approach in determining what can be inferred from the text of a patent application than foreign patent offices. However, for applications filed in foreign countries, the claim language needs to mimic the language in the specification to a greater degree than patent applications filed in the United States. In other words, the claim limitations that a patent applicant may want to include in a claim after its initial filing must essentially be found word-for-word within the Detailed Description of the patent application when prosecuting foreign patent application. Even though the U.S. takes a more liberal approach, the drafter should strive to make explicit aspects of the invention that the inventor wants to claim in light of possible foreign patent prosecution. This should be done in the event that the patent application is filed in foreign countries that have a strict approach to what information can be included in the amendments made to claims.

Writing Tip #3:
Using the word "may" versus "is"

The claims define the scope of patent protection. Every word or phrase of a claim limits the scope of its protection and, during litigation, the court strives to give every word in each claim a meaning.[40] When a potential infringer is being sued, the court takes every word into account, and the more that the invention, or one of its components, is described as being equal to something (i.e., that it "is" something), the courts will hold the patent owner to his or her own statements. Such language makes it harder for a potential infringer to be held liable if the alleged infringing device does not exactly match the description of the invention in the patent application. Phrases such as "may be" qualify statements made in the patent application and mitigate this issue.

The invention should therefore be described as, for example, "may be" having certain features as opposed to "is," "having", or "as having" those features. For example: the "mechanical clicker may be fabricated from a plastic material, but other similarly rigid material is also contemplated." The reason is that, as has been explained before, the description sections of the patent application serve as a dictionary for terms in the Claims Set and a means by which the claims are interpreted. If the patent application describes the invention or its components as "is" something, the courts are more likely to construe the claims as *requiring* that characteristic when defining the scope of patent protection. If an accused infringer does not incorporate that "essential" characteristic, there would be no patent infringement and thus no patent infringement liability. However, when "may" is used to describe the invention's features, the courts are less likely to construe the claims as requiring such features as essential to the invention when defining the scope of patent protection.

For example, in *Cadence Pharmaceutical v. Exela Pharm Sci Inc.*,[41] in which the patent owner (Cadence) sued the accused infringer (Exela) for patent infringement, the court had to give a meaning to the term "buffering agent" in the claims of Cadence's patent to determine whether infringement existed. Cadence's patent specification included potentially narrowing statements in relation to the concentration of the buffering agent as being between

0.1 and 10 mg/ml. However, the court did not construe the "buffering agent" limitation as limited to those specific concentration levels, because the patent specification stated they "may be" between 0.1 and 10 mg/ml. If the term "is" had taken the place of "may be" in this case, the court may have interpreted the buffering agent claim more narrowly, and Cadence may have lost its case against the infringer.

As discussed previously, specifics such as what the concentration of this buffering agent *may be* provide a backup argument for patentability downstream during examination so that claims can be narrowed if necessary. However, there is the potential for those specifics to be interpreted in such a way as to limit the claim, as illustrated by the *Cadence* case. To mitigate this possibility, the invention or aspects thereof should be described in terms of what the invention "may be" and not what the invention "is," just as Cadence did. The more that the application states that an invention "is" something, the more likely it is that the courts will include that characteristic as a required limitation in the claims. However, stating that an aspect of the invention "may be" something mitigates the possibility that the courts will narrowly interpret the patent's claims.

Writing Tip #4:
Preferred embodiments and using the word "substantial"

Using non-committal terms such as "preferred" and "substantially" broadens the description and claim language. Stating that an embodiment of an invention is "preferred" implies that the inventor has contemplated variations, but thinks this version is best.

The usefulness of broadening claims with these terms is illustrated in the case of *Verderi, LLC v. Google, Inc.*[42] Verderi (patent owner) sued Google for patent infringement, complaining that Google's "Street View" infringed on its own patented technology that was directed to providing synthesized images of a geographic area that a user navigates online. In Google's application, the internet user can pan left, right, up, and down to view the surrounding scenery. Google's infringement hinged on whether Verderi's claim, which included the phrase "substantial elevations,"[43] meant that only vertically *flat* depictions of the objects were protected by the patent, or that "substantially elevations" could also include *curved or spherical* depictions. The District Court construed the phrase as excluding[44] curved or spherical depictions of the objects. Since Google's Street View included spherical depictions, the District Court granted summary judgment in favor of Google, which was found to not infringe Verderi's patent claims.

On appeal, the Federal Circuit reversed this ruling, deciding that the District Court had erroneously interpreted Verderi's claims as excluding the possibility of curved or spherical depictions even though the specification and prosecution history of Verderi's patents had allowed for the possibility of curved or spherical depictions. In addition, the patent owner did not clearly disavow inclusion of curved or spherical depictions due to their use of the adverb "substantially." This term reflected an intent to include something more than just an elevation view, namely, curved or spherical depictions. The Federal Circuit reasoned that the word "substantially" broadened the term "elevation" to include curved or spherical depictions, reversed the District Court's claim construction, vacated its judgment of non-infringement, and remanded for further consideration. In this instance, the claim was considered sufficiently broad to encompass Google's "Street View" and was saved because the term "substantially" modified the term "elevation" to include more than its strict, architectural sense, namely, curved and spherical depictions.

Writing Tip #5:
Do not use the word, "invention"

Use of the word "invention" when drafting a patent application is a natural tendency but a disfavored practice because it may narrow patent protection. In the past when patents repeatedly state that an "invention" is "X," courts have sometimes gone to great lengths to construe the claims such that "X" is required, thereby narrowing the scope of patent protection.

The importance of not using the term "invention" is exemplified in the case of *Pacing Technologies, LLC. v. Garmin International, Inc.*[45] in which Pacing technologies (patent owner) sued Garmin for patent infringement on a device that recorded a user's pace while running, walking, or cycling. The claims at issue did not expressly require the device to emit a sensible tempo (e.g., light, sound, etc.,). However, because the patent used the word "invention and associated the invention with a sensible tempo, the Federal Circuit went to great lengths to interpret the claim language as implicitly requiring a sensible tempo for patent infringement to be established. In particular, the patent owner listed several "objects of the invention," stating the device was "adapted to producing a sensible tempo." Therefore, the court read the specification as a clear disavowal of all versions of the invention that did not include a "sensible tempo" and concluded that the claimed invention must include the "sensible tempo" feature.

Garmin (the defendant) had included a type of pacing feature in its products. Garmin's watch displayed a runner's target pace and immediately next to that, the actual pace of the wearer was displayed as well. The wearer could visually compare the two pace numbers (i.e., target and actual paces) to quickly determine whether he or she is faster or slower than the target pace. However, Garmin did not incorporate an audible indication into its watch, and thus no "sensible tempo. Since the Federal Circuit ruled that Pacing Technologies' patent required a "sensible tempo," they found Garmin's product did not infringe on Pacing Technologies' patent and Garmin was not liable for patent infringement.

Broad characterizations of an invention as a whole in the patent application may not be beneficial. It is generally better to highlight one unique aspect of the device or method rather than to describe the invention as unique due to a given feature. For example, a unique type of engine (e.g., rotary engine) that happens to be in a car is distinct from a car that is unique because it has a rotary engine. In the case of the former, the rotary engine is the invention and any device including a rotary engine would infringe on its patent. In the case of the latter, the car is the invention and any device that is not a car, regardless of the incorporation of a rotary engine, would not infringe on the patent. Refocusing the invention's definition from the car to the engine broadens the patent's specification and its claims.

As has been shown, it is best not to use of the word "invention" in the patent specification. In most instances, the word "invention" can be replaced with the terms "device," "method," "system," "apparatus," or "one aspect of the device or method," and retain the same essential meaning. In this way, the statements in the patent specification are more flexible since they would not describe objects of the invention, which could inadvertently narrow the definition of the invention.

Writing Tip #6:
Suboptimal embodiments

It may be beneficial to include suboptimal embodiments (i.e., versions of the invention that are not what the inventor understands to be its best mode) in the patent application along with alternative embodiments of the invention that are not central to the inventor's vision, at least to the extent that they relate to the point of novelty. If the mechanical pencil's point of novelty is the mechanism that pushes the lead forward through the pencil (i.e., the mechanical clicker), the mechanical clicker's optimal positioning, and best mode, may be near the user's index finger. However, indicating that the mechanical clicker can be positioned at different, less convenient areas (e.g., upper part near the eraser) of the pencil body may also be beneficial. Less optimal embodiments may not be as advantageous those of the best mode of the mechanical pencil, but can nevertheless be considered a minimally viable product that could compete with the invention. Hence, the minimally viable product or embodiment should be included in the patent application with the claims directed to the shared point of novelty to secure proper patent protection (in this case, a mechanical clicker positioned on the body of the mechanical pencil regardless of its position). Including these alternative embodiments also provides a buffer zone around the preferred embodiments of the invention by preventing others from obtaining a patent on these alternative embodiments. For example, including multiple, though less convenient, positions of the mechanical clicker system in the patent application would prevent others from patenting a mechanical pencil that is only slightly different such as a mechanical pencil with a clicker system on a different position away from the index finger on the pencil body.

As a case in point for including suboptimal embodiments, Kennametal (patent owner) sued Ingersoll (accused infringer) for patent infringement on its patented cutting tool containing ruthenium as a binder, which was coated onto the tool using a physical vapor deposition (PVD) process.[46] Ingersoll attacked the patent's validity, citing a prior art reference in a another company's (Grab) patent in which the application of the ruthenium coating by way of physical vapor disposition was not the primary way of applying the coating. However, it had been included as a passing comment and appears to have been an afterthought during the preparation of the patent application.[47] The court ruled Kennametal's patent invalid and that the teaching or disclosure found in the Grab prior art reference prevented other companies from securing a patent for the process of applying ruthenium as a binder via PVD.

Based on *Kennametal,* use of the phrase, "other ways or means or components are also contemplated including but not limited to [insert list of alternatives]," may be used to broaden the scope of patent protection. This case also demonstrates the advantages of including alternative embodiments to prevent others from securing a patent on similar, yet distinct (and perhaps less effective), methods. At the time of filing, the inventor may consider them less favorable, but one may later become the preferred embodiment, or at least a competitive alternative.

By including these alternative embodiments in the application, prior art is created that can be used against the patents and patent applications of competitors. Moreover, by including them in the specification, the inventor is able to later claim these alternative embodiments for him or herself.

Writing Tip #7:
Ranges

When filing a patent application for inventions that include ranges (e.g., percentages, quantities, or temperatures) such as pharmaceuticals, compositions, or processes, the purpose of the ranges should be included. This may be important for overcoming a prior art reference.

For example, in *Ineos USA LLC v. Berry Plastic Corp.,*[48] Ineos (patent owner) sued Berry Plastic (accused infringer) for patent infringement on its polyethylene based compositions, which was used to form shaped products such as screw caps for bottles. To optimize the cap's slip properties, manufacturers would typically add a lubricant. Unfortunately, the lubricant added an unpleasant odor or flavor to the food product. Ineos' invented a composition with specific amounts of polyethylene, lubricants, and additives. This composition solved these odor and flavor problems. Ineos presented claims for the invention in terms of these various components but within certain percentages by weight.

The defendant (Berry), attempting to invalidate the patent as not novel, brought forth a prior art reference that disclosed all the components but with slightly different ranges. Since Ineos did not include why its range was so critical for its anti-slip properties while not affecting the smell or taste of the product, the Federal Circuit found that the prior art reference anticipated or disclosed all the limitations of the claimed invention.

As this case demonstrates, it may be important to indicate, if possible, how operability and functionality of the claimed invention changes within the range. Including the reason for a particular range is critical to the invention and may be helpful to overcome prior art references that disclose an overlapping range. Unfortunately, this information is often obtained through testing, which may be costly or time-consuming to carry out before the patent application is filed but would be very helpful to include in the patent application.

Writing Tip #8:
Software Inventions

The extent to which software inventions should be eligible for patent protection is currently under debate. Since 2014, patent applications identified as directed to "software" have received a significantly lower allowance rate than other inventions because they are considered abstract ideas under 35 U.S.C. 101 (see Appendix F), and thus are ineligible for patent protection.

If a patent application is prepared and filed for software or a device that relies heavily on software as the point of novelty, the patent application should disclose the algorithm (i.e., the software's structure) that describes how to perform a function claimed in the Claim Set. There is no required format, but the algorithm should be expressed in a way that communicates the software's structure.[49]

In *Augme Technologies v. Yahoo* the patent claim referred to "code assembler instructions" with only a black box in a diagram of the patent and no instructions on how to assemble the code (see 238 in Figure 7, below).[50] If the patent does not disclose the algorithm of the claimed step, the patent is deemed indefinite. In this case, the court invalidated the patent claims because no algorithm was disclosed. Figures 7 and 8 below show the diagrams and their descriptions included in the patent. They illustrate what is *not* sufficient for disclosing a software algorithm.

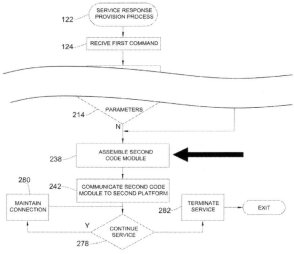

Figure 7

USPN 6594691 col. 11, ln. 60-col. 12, ln 1.

11

Task **238** causes processor **62** to execute code assembler 60 instructions **86** (FIG. 1) to assemble second code module **90**. Second code module **90** is assembled by accessing the predetrmined one of denial of service response **162** (FIG. 7), conditional service response **176**(FIG. 7), and predeter- 65 mined service response **186** (FIG.7) from Web address database **68**. In addition, second code module **90** is assembled in response to browse information **56** and plat-

12

form information **58**. In other words, second code module **90** is assembled to include the service response and to work with any combination of browser/platform systems. This feature eliminates the need for an affiliate program to 5 be hard coded, installed onto Web page **34**, then tested and

4

50 database instructions **82** are executed by processor **62** for maintaining and accessing visitor database **70**. CGI interface program **84** executes functions as server system **26** including among other things, checking if web site **34** is registered. Code assembler instructions **86** are executed by processor **62** 55 to assemble a second code module **90** which is subsequently communicated to second processor platform **24** through the execution of CGI interface program **84** and communication instructions **88**. Second code module **90** is communicated from ports **78** over Internet **28** and downloaded to temporary 50 memory **54** at second processor platform **24**.

Figure 8

The court stated that the verbiage in the specification explains that the "code assembler instructions" do the assembling and discloses inputs to, and outputs from, the code assembler instruction. However, the specification was lacking any algorithm for how the second code module is actually assembled. Simply disclosing that the black box performs a recited function is not a sufficient explanation of the algorithm required to render the claim term definite. The court is looking for something more than just a generic description. It cannot merely be stated that the second code module is assembled by "accessing" something. Merely "accessing" does not instruct someone how to assemble the second code module. Rather, the court is looking for specific instructions on how the second code module is actually assembled. Inventors that decide to pursue a software patent need to include the specific process of the software, or the patent (which is hard to obtain in the first place) will likely not be granted.

Section 3

Patent Prosecution FAQs

This section addresses issues and questions that I commonly encounter as I represent inventors and guide them through the patent prosecution process. Patent prosecution refers to the process of shepherding a patent application through the USPTO's process from the time the patent application is filed to its maturation. Understanding these, sometimes counterintuitive, steps will enable inventors to utilize them for their own benefit. My goal is both to explain the rules and procedures of the patent prosecution process and, more importantly, to help inventors understand how to take advantage of the rules and procedures for their own benefit.

FAQ #1:
How long will it take to get a patent? Is there any way to speed up the process?

Normal wait time: One to three years or longer

It normally takes one to three years, or longer, for a filed, nonprovisional patent application to be examined.[51] However, the process can be expedited so that substantive examination of the patent application occurs within six months. Generally, I do not recommend expedited examination without good business or personal reason because the initial Office Action will be rendered earlier and applicants will incur substantial patent prosecution costs (i.e., the examination costs) earlier in the patent process. Delaying attorney fees may be beneficial for a startup, solo inventor, or investor as this allows them to test marketing first before spending more on legal fees, and requesting expedited examination is therefore not recommended.

Some clients do not need the issued patent during the early stages of their business launches and do not request expedited examination. Some entrepreneurs have existing business relationships, distribution channels, and/or customers so a patent is not essential to the success of their product. In these cases, clients would rather wait for the USPTO to render the initial Office Action since the issued patent is a small part of their long-range business plans. By contrast, other clients may seek a patent earlier to attract investors and licensees. The issuance of the patent could significantly enhance the attractiveness of the invention to investors and also to potential licensees. These clients may choose to expedite examination and incur the expenses sooner rather than later to secure the patent.[52]

Usually the USPTO examines patent applications in the order in which they are received. By applying for expedited examination, an application can be examined before those that were submitted prior to it. Two common procedures for requesting expedited examination are "prioritized examination" (i.e., "Track One") and a petition "to make special based on age." There are other forms of expedited examination, but these are not available or beneficial to most applicants.

Speeding up the process: Prioritized examination, or, Track One request

The Track One request was borne out of inventors' frustrations regarding the monetary and business costs associated with delayed examination, which in some cases prevented inventors from exploiting their inventions immediately. The Track One request enables an applicant to pay for the advantage of expedited examination of his or her patent application if they believe that delayed prosecution really does cost them money. Prioritized examination costs about one to four thousand dollars for the governmental fees alone and depends on the size (i.e., micro-entity small entity, or large entity) of the business or entity (i.e., Applicant).[53] The Track One request must be filed at the time of filing the nonprovisional patent application. When a patent application is filed with a prioritized examination request, the USPTO typically renders an initial Office Action in less than six months, as opposed to the usual fourteen months.

Speeding up the process: Petition to make special based on age

A petition to "make special based on age" is free but at least one of the inventors must be sixty-five years of age or older. The petition is a single page form that can be filled out after the nonprovisional patent application has been filed and any time before the USTPO issues the first Office Action. If a petition to make special based on age is granted, the first substantive Office Action may be rendered in as early as six months. However, it has been my experience that these types of requests are not closely tracked by the USPTO, and thus patent counsel should follow up with the USPTO to make sure that the petition has been calendared on the examiner's docket.[54]

FAQ #2:
What does the patent application process cost? If I take a do-it-yourself (DIY) approach to drafting my patent application, will it save me money?

Invest in a competent attorney upfront and you will save time and money in the end

As discussed in Chapter 9, I recommend retaining a competent patent attorney to draft the application and respond to Office Actions rather than taking a DIY approach. This will ultimately save time and money. The documents involved are complicated and should be handled by a professional. If not handled by a professional, an inventor might create problems that prevent securing a patent on the invention, are expensive to fix, or are not possible to fix. Utilizing the services of patent counsel will mitigate these issues.

A patent attorney will discuss costs and fees during the initial consultation. The costs and fees associated with the preparation and filing of a patent application with the USPTO is contingent on various factors discussed in detail in Chapter 9. *Costs* are related to out-of-pocket costs of preparing, filing, or representing the client in the patent matter. For example, money paid to prepare a drawing set is a cost. Money paid to the government for receiving and processing the patent application is a cost. By contrast, a *fee* is typically associated with the time an attorney requires to represent, advise, and prepare applications for a client. The time required to perform these tasks is multiplied by the attorney's billing rate, and that price is a fee.

Costs and fees vary significantly according to the complexity of the invention and the breadth of protection desired. Even if the invention appears to be simple and straightforward, it may be somewhat difficult to prepare because we are trying to illustrate an invention's uniqueness in the patent application. That is harder to do for simple inventions. Therefore work required for a simple invention would be costlier than expected. (See Chapter 9 regarding the relative costs of provisional and nonprovisional patent applications.)

FAQ #3:
What exactly am I paying for when I hire a patent attorney?

Experience, experience, experience.

The primary benefits of hiring a patent attorney are experience, know- how, and strategies that the patent attorney has accumulated over the years and utilized to help others in the inventor's situation. Competent patent counsel can guide you through the process, keep you focused on the task at hand, listen to your business situation, provide a next-steps plan, and spot problematic issues that may need to be resolved beforehand. A patent attorney will organize the information regarding the invention, draft the patent application, and prosecute it before the USPTO.

When hiring a patent attorney, the costs and fees depend on the client's needs as well as the solutions developed by the attorney. Some alternatives are more expensive than others. Although clients generally prefer the least expensive option, competent patent counsel should provide a number of potential resolutions along with their pros and cons to guide an inventor through the patent process and help them make an informed decision in the matter.

Instead of selecting a patent attorney according to cost, I generally recommend that the inventor select an attorney on the attorney's ability to craft a strategy for securing patent protection. With their training and experience, attorneys should be able to identify the options of greatest value for the client. As such, a potential client may want to ask about a particular aspect of the attorney's strategy for protecting an invention such as a claiming strategy when interviewing a patent attorney.

In my practice, for example, I generally recommend that startups seek meaningful, medium-sized claims instead of broad patent protection (i.e., broad claims). Why? Because broad claims are expensive. The attorney must generally prepare multiple responses to multiple Office Actions. Narrow patent protection, on the other hand, requires less work from the attorney and is less expensive, but may offer minimal protection. Startups are generally less well-funded and cannot seek very broad patent protection. Startups are generally satisfied therefore if they can launch a product with meaningful, medium breadth protection that would dissuade competitors from entering their specific market. This would be a cost-effective way to seek patent protection in the short term. It is important when searching for a patent attorney to seek someone who can articulate a claiming strategy and a strategy for cost effectively building out the client's patent portfolio that fits the client's needs and will deliver the most reasonable cost-value balance for their services.

FAQ #4:
Do I have a duty to search prior art before I file my patent application?

No, but if you do, you must disclose your results to the USPTO!

An inventor does not have a duty to search prior art before filing a patent application. However, if an inventor has conducted a formal or informal search, the references uncovered in the search should be disclosed. Also, anyone involved in the preparation and filing of a patent application has a duty to disclose what they may already know about the prior art.

The patent examination procedure at the USPTO is not an adversarial system as a lawsuit is. Rather, it is a cooperative investigation between the examiner and an applicant. The examiner is supposed to act as an advocate for the public and not as an adversary to inventors. Because the patent examination process is not an adversarial system, the USPTO places this duty of disclosure on the patent applicant. It is the patent applicant's duty to disclose material information to the USPTO regarding the invention so that the patent examiner can determine whether to grant or reject the claimed invention for patent.[55] Because examination is a cooperative investigation, the rules impose on the patent applicant a duty of candor and good faith in dealing with the USPTO.

Should there be litigation and known material information was not disclosed, a court could render the patent invalid based on inequitable conduct due to the failure to meet the duty of disclosure and of candor and good faith. It is therefore recommended to take a liberal approach and disclose any reference that may be relevant to the invention, as there is no benefit of withholding potentially relevant information. If the patent application matures into a patent after disclosing the information to the examiner, the benefit of liberally disclosing information is that the patent will be presumed valid over that information or reference. The inventor can satisfy the duty of disclosure by filing an Information Disclosure Statement (IDS; See Chapter 7 for more information on the IDS).[56]

FAQ #5:
What happens after the patent application is filed with the USPTO?

A review of formal requirements by the Office of Initial Patent Examination

After filing a patent application with the USPTO, the Office of Initial Patent Examination (OIPE) will review the patent application to determine whether the application fulfills formalities such as providing an application data sheet (ADS), declaration(s), power of attorney, and other required documents. The OIPE will also review the patent application to determine whether the drawings conform to USPTO standards. The OIPE determines whether the patent application meets, in general terms, the formal requirements of the patent application.

If the OIPE finds any deficiencies, it will request that the applicant correct them. After the patent application passes OIPE examination, it is assigned to a patent examiner whose background is related to the invention's subject matter. The patent examiner will review the patent application and search the prior art to determine whether the invention meets the substantive patent requirements and then allow or reject the application. For more information about rejections, see the section below on dealing with rejections, namely, see FAQ #17-21.

FAQ #6:
Can my competitors see the content of my patent application? Is there any way to keep them in the dark about its contents and its progress in the patent prosecution process?

Yes, and yes (if you don't file for a patent in foreign countries)!

Startups and solo inventors often ask whether others can see the content of their patent application. When patent applications are filed, they are kept secret initially, but will eventually become published prior to the issuance of the patent. The information in the patent application will therefore eventually be accessible to others. Inventors are often concerned about keeping their inventions secret prior to the filing of the patent application. After the filing, the invention has "patent pending" status. It is therefore safe to disclose the invention or the patent pending product through marketing efforts after filing the patent application because anyone that seeks a patent based on your marketing efforts would have filed their patent application after yours.

However, there are instances in which it is advantageous to prevent competitors from learning about the information included in the patent application. For example, the patent application may contain additional information over and above the basic invention such as alternative embodiments, the minimally viable product, and other details regarding the point of novelty. In some cases, it is in the inventor's best interest to keep these secret for as long as possible (i.e., until the patent application matures into a patent). This can be done by making a nonpublication request when filing. This request will ensure the secrecy of the contents of the patent application until (or if) the patent is granted.[57] However, for a patent applicant to file a nonpublication request, the inventor must be able to declare that he or she has no intent to file a patent application in foreign countries.[58]

FAQ #7:
What is the relationship between a nonpublication request and preserving the ability to file for patent protection in foreign countries?

If you file a nonpublication request, you cannot file for patent protection in foreign countries

Requests for nonpublication and preservation of the ability to file in foreign countries are interrelated. If an applicant intends to file patent applications in foreign countries, filing a request for nonpublication is not possible. Conversely, if the applicant does not intend to file patent applications in foreign countries, the applicant can file a request for nonpublication. The request for nonpublication is a box that can be checked on the Application Data Sheet, which is filed with the patent application. If the applicant later decides to file a patent application in any foreign country, the patent applicant may file a revocation of the request for nonpublication within forty-five days of filing the patent application in another country or filing a PCT application.

FAQ #8:
Should I consider filing for foreign patent protection?

Only if you have established business ties in foreign countries or another good reason to do so

Because foreign filing is expensive, I generally do not recommend that small businesses, startups, or solo inventors do so unless they have viable plan to profit from it. Profiting in foreign markets in the future without current existing business relationships, distribution channels, etc., in foreign countries is possible, but not common, in my experience. It may take years to build necessary relationships that can be financially exploited for a profit. By the time a startup would establish foreign relationships, it would begin incurring annuities[59] to maintain the pendency of the patent application and would therefore divert funds away from operations in the United States, which makes financial success in the U.S. difficult.

FAQ #9:
How much does it cost to secure foreign patent protection?

Not much to preserve your right to do so, but a lot to secure foreign patents.

As discussed in Chapter 6, there is no initial cost to preserve the ability to file patent applications in foreign countries. An inventor only needs to file a patent application in the United States before engaging in marketing activities. An applicant must file utility patent applications in any foreign country within twelve months after filing a utility patent application, or after six months for design patent applications.

The twelve-month deadline to file utility patent applications in a foreign country may be extended another eighteen months by filing a Patent Cooperation Treaty (PCT) application. A PCT application gives an applicant up to thirty months from the initial filing of the patent application to file in foreign countries.[60] The PCT application does not apply to design patent applications.

Instead of filing the PCT application, a patent application can be filed directly in foreign countries, but it can be quite expensive because of annuities. Many foreign, patent office's require an annuity (i.e., an annual payment) to the foreign patent office to maintain the pendency of the patent application. They range between a few hundred to a few thousand dollars each year. There are also annual maintenance fees to maintain issued patents in force.

If a business needs to seek foreign patent protection, the entrepreneur can file the PCT application and, within the thirty-month period, actively establish foreign business relationships or licensees that already have those foreign business relationships. The thirty-month period is crucial because at the end of thirty months, the business will have to file patent applications directly in each individual foreign country, which may be cost prohibitive without any assurance that the business will be profitable in those foreign countries.

FAQ #10:
What is a restriction requirement?

A mandate from the examiner to divide your claims into more than one category and elect one for examination

A "restriction requirement" is an examiner's decision that the claims of the patent application are directed to two or more separate and independent inventions (i.e., categories) and that the patent applicant must choose one of those inventions for examination. The examiner will not examine a Claim Set directed to two or more inventions. For example, claims to the product (i.e., apparatus claims) and claims to the method of using the product may be considered two different inventions and therefore subject to a restriction requirement.

Claims directed to alternative embodiments and other aspects of the invention might also be considered wholly different inventions. For example, inventions related to a transmitter-receiver system may include claims directed to a receiver, different claims directed to a transmitter, or claims directed to the system of the receiver and transmitter. Claims directed to the receiver in contrast to claims directed to the transmitter may be considered different inventions. In this case, an examiner may render a restriction requirement and, as in the example above, the applicant would need to choose between the claims directed to the receiver, transmitter, or system including the transmitter and receiver. Inventors might think of all these components as elements of one single invention, but they may likely be three, legally different inventions, as discussed below.

FAQ #11:
What are common situations in which a restriction requirement is made?

When both an apparatus and a method claim are included in the Claim Set

Restriction requirements are frequently made when Claim Sets recite both an apparatus claim and a method claim. Additionally, if a patent application admits that there are multiple embodiments, the examiner may be more likely to render the restriction requirement and divide the application based on how the application describes the multiple embodiments. Even though these aspects might cause an examiner to render a restriction requirement, inventors should not exclude them from the patent application when deciding what to include in the patent application. They should discuss whether including these aspects in their patent application would be beneficial with their patent attorney.

FAQ #12:
Why is the examiner saying that there are two or more inventions in the patent application and asking me to select only one for examination?

Technical, legal definitions and reasoning

In my experience, inventors often feel examiners are incorrect in rendering restriction requirements. They do not feel the product and its method of use are different inventions. For example, the transmitter claims and the receiver claims do not appear to be different inventions. Although from a layperson's perspective this may seem correct, the legal definition used by the USPTO to determine when claims are directed to two or more inventions is very broad and differs from a lay understanding.

Often from the layperson's standpoint, the product claim and the method claim for the product's use are the same invention since they refer to the same apparatus. However, if the apparatus can be used with two or more methods, as is often the case, the scope of examination for the method and apparatus claims are not co-extensive and are therefore different inventions. For example, a kitchen knife can be used in two different methods. A first method entails using the knife to slice tomato. A second method of using the knife entails crushing garlic. In this regard, the knife claim may be considered a different invention from a method claim involving the knife.

FAQ #13:
Should I choose the apparatus or the method claims when there is a restriction requirement between the two?

It is usually best to choose the apparatus claim for examination.

For a restriction requirement based on the apparatus and method claims, it is usually more beneficial to select the apparatus claims for examination because they are generally broader than method claims. Apparatus claims cover all methods of use whereas a method claim covers only one. However, there are cases in which one might want to select the narrower method claims for examination. For example, if the goal is to seek the issuance of a patent regardless of the scope of protection, it would be preferable to have the method claims examined because they are theoretically harder to reject than an apparatus claim. The inventor can always seek broader patent protection by filing one or more continuing patent applications, as discussed below (FAQ#22-29).

FAQ #14:
Can I still secure a patent for non-elected claims in response to a restriction requirement?

Yes!

Restriction requirements do not prevent applicants from seeking examination on non-elected inventions. A restriction requirement simply indicates that the examiner will examine only the elected invention. The non-elected invention(s) can be examined in a subsequent application (i.e., continuing application). A continuing application may be filed at any time before the current patent application is either abandoned or a patent is issued. An applicant can file a continuing application immediately or wait to see how the current patent application proceeds through the examination stage.[61]

FAQ #15:
Should I oppose the examiner (i.e., "traverse" the examiner's position) on the restriction requirement?

I generally do not recommend it.

The restriction requirement may be "traversed" but is usually costly and unsuccessful. Even if an applicant traverses a restriction requirement, the USPTO requires the applicant to select one of the claimed inventions for examination so that patent prosecution can continue should the examiner not withdraw the restriction requirement. Unless there is a clear error in the restriction requirement, I generally do not recommend traversing it because it is rarely successful, and it is generally less expensive to file continuing patent application to secure patent protection for the non-elected claims.

FAQ #16:
Are there any benefits to not traversing the restriction requirement?

A restriction requirement might not be as bad as you think.

In my opinion, a restriction requirement is not detrimental to the examination. It may even be beneficial. The non-elected claims can be examined in a divisional application, and the examiner cannot render a "nonstatutory double patenting rejection."[62] A nonstatutory double patent rejection occurs if the claims of the patent application are similar, but not identical, to a pending patent application or an issued patent. To overcome a nonstatutory double patenting rejection, the inventor can file a terminal disclaimer that disclaims any "terminal portion" of the patent maturing from the divisional application that extends beyond the patent term of the previously filed patent application. In this case, the parent and divisional patent applications will have "co-extensive patent terms."

If a restriction requirement is made, a nonstatutory double patenting rejection cannot be made. Thus, the terms of the patents maturing from patent applications having a common parent application may be different. This means the inventor might have a patent term for one of the patents that is longer than the other patent,[63] which could be beneficial for inventions that have significant, daily, commercial value. For example, some patented pharmaceuticals are worth millions of dollars per day and it might be advantageous to extend the patent term even by one day. Other inventions are worth less money, but the patent owner may nonetheless wish to retain the possibility to extend the patent term if the benefits outweigh the costs.

FAQ #17:
Was there a mistake in the preparation or filing of my patent application if there is a rejection or notice is made to correct the formalities of the patent application?

No, it is likely just a normal part of the patent process.

A rejection or notice to correct informalities does not indicate that a mistake exists in the patent application. In fact, many patent applications are rejected for not meeting formal and/ or informal requirements. Rejections can be rendered even after a formal patent search has been conducted and no prior art reference has been found that anticipates the invention. It could have been that the patent search failed to find the most relevant prior art reference, which was then found by the examiner. Even in this situation, there is not necessarily a mistake in the patent application. As explained in Chapter 3, a novelty search does not guarantee that a patent application will mature into an official patent, but merely indicate the likelihood of a result.

FAQ #18:
What are the most common office action rejections?

Novelty and non-obviousness

The most common, substantive rejections are related to novelty and "non-obviousness."[64] Other substantive requirements include, but are not limited to, written description and enablement, but those will not be discussed in great length here.[65] Novelty requires that the invention be new and not already in existence. If the invention is not new, the United States government has no incentive to award a patent for it. The public already has access to the information held by the inventor. Non- obviousness requires that an invention be more than a mere, obvious variant of existing technology. An invention that is an obvious variant is, by definition, likely to be introduced by someone else to the public. The United States government has no incentive to award a patent for an obvious invention because it would otherwise, inevitably become known to the public. If your invention is non-obvious, the public benefits from it only by the inventor's public disclosure of it. Granting patents is meant to motivate inventors to disclose novel and non-obvious inventions to the public.

FAQ #19:
Why is my invention being rejected, especially if it is a more advanced than the cited prior art?

It is all about the claims!

The invention is being rejected because the *claimed invention*, not the *disclosure* (i.e., the entire specification, including both the text and drawings in the application), is not novel compared to the prior art. The claimed invention is defined only by that which is in the Claim Set. Only the claims are considered when rejecting an invention. The invention may be more advanced than the prior art, but the claims may be written so broadly as to encompass prior art references cited by the examiner and therefore not considered to be novel.

An examiner attempts to find a single document (i.e., primary art reference) that teaches all the elements or limitations recited in a claim. If one reference cannot be found that discloses all limitations of the claimed invention, the examiner may combine other documents (i.e., secondary references) and argue that the claimed invention is an obvious variant of the primary reference. That is, an examiner asserts that a person of ordinary skill in the art would have been motivated to modify the primary reference in conjunction with the secondary reference(s) to come up with the claimed invention.

FAQ #20:
Why is the examiner rejecting the claims based on unrelated prior art?

The Broadest Reasonable Interpretation (BRI) standard gives the examiner considerable leeway to determine analogous prior art.

It may appear that the examiner is rejecting the claimed invention based on prior art that seems irrelevant to the claimed invention. However, the examiner is most likely making a reasonable rejection. Under the BRI standard, the examiner can interpret every word written in a claim with the broadest reasonable interpretation. For example, a "foot support" for a human powered vehicle could be a pedal or a skateboard deck. When an examiner searches through prior art, even if the invention is directed to a skateboard, the examiner may be searching prior art related to bicycles, tricycles, and other wheeled vehicles because they too include what could be considered a "foot support. The concept of the broadest reasonable interpretation gives the examiner great leeway in construing the claims. Unless an applicant appeals the examiner's interpretation to the Patent, Trademark, and Appeal Board (PTAB), they should amend the language of the claims so that the language of the claims does not allow the examiner to interpret the claims so broadly.

In sum, the BRI standard significantly broadens the possible scope of the claimed invention during patent prosecution for examination purposes so that the examiner can consequently use what appears to be unrelated prior art to reject the claimed invention. An examiner could therefore reject the claim based on technology that is wholly unrelated to the invention. For example, an examiner may utilize prior art references related to fake concrete in rejecting an invention directed to technology for real concrete. The inventor may erroneously feel as if the examiner does not understand the invention or believe the patent application was written incorrectly because the legal definition of prior art is much broader than what the inventor usually feels is analogous or related.

A reference can be used to reject an invention for obviousness if it is an analogous art.[66] A reference is analogous art to the claimed invention if: (1) the references from the same field of endeavor as the claimed invention (even if it addresses a different problem), or (2) the references are reasonably pertinent to the problem faced by the inventor (even if it is not in the same field of endeavor at the claimed invention). To have the reference withdrawn as prior art, the applicant could argue that the reference is non-analogous prior art based on the definition given above. However, in practice, even if the cited prior art is non-analogous, it is hard to convince the examiner to withdraw a reference for being non- analogous prior art.

It would be usually easier to argue that a non-analogous reference contains information that a person of ordinary skill in the art (e.g., real concrete) would be taught away from using or implementing the teachings in art that is non-analogous (e.g., fake concrete reference), making the invention non-obvious. Non-obviousness arguments are easier to make and are stronger arguments for patentability than arguing that the reference is non-analogous art.

FAQ #21:
The patent application has been rejected on substantive grounds. Should I give up on the process?

It depends... how is the invention doing in the marketplace?

The decision to end the patent examination process is a hard one and is dictated by many different factors such as whether the invention is doing well in the marketplace and whether the arguments for patentability are strong.

If the invention is not doing well in the marketplace, the likelihood of the patent application maturing into a patent probably does not matter. In such cases, the costs and effort associated with the patent examination process should probably be abandoned to minimize legal costs. If the invention is doing very well in the marketplace, the likelihood that the patent application will mature into a patent is moot as well. The inventor must continue with the examination process because the patent application provides the only vehicle by which an inventor can block others, including large companies that are well-funded and have extensive marketing networks in the marketplace. The patent application equalizes such inequalities between startup businesses and large companies. Deciding to abandon the patent process is harder if the invention's performance in the marketplace is mediocre because discontinuing the patent process may mean giving up on the business

If the arguments for patentability are weak based on the prior art references and the examiner's rejection, it may be time to consider giving up on the examination process to mitigate the legal costs. However, all options should be analyzed before doing so because all patent rights could be irreversibly dedicated to the public upon abandonment and the inventor may lose the ability to secure a patent.

FAQ #22:
Can I broaden my patent?

It's complicated.

Once a patent application matures into a patent, the scope of patent protection, as defined by the patent claims, is fixed. Patent owners generally want to broaden protection if the existing patent does not include claims that stop inventors from competing against the patent owner. The scope of the claims cannot be broadened except for a few, post-grant procedures such as a "broadening re-issue application". However, the broadening amendments that can be made to the claims in the broadening re-issue application are limited and may be insufficient to secure a claim broad enough to encompass the competitor's product.

FAQ #23:
How does the continuation practice work to broaden patent protection of my invention?

Filing serial continuing applications slowly broadens the scope of patent protections

Although the scope of patent protection afforded under a patent is fixed, it is possible to seek broader patent protection for an invention through a continuing application, known as "continuation practice." Continuation practice refers to a practice of serially filing continuing applications that claim priority to a previous, nonprovisional application to broaden the portfolio of patents. Through this process, the subject matter disclosed in a patent application can remain pending for up to twenty years from the filing of the original application or first, nonprovisional patent application.

This practice enables the patent applicant to obtain a patent for the invention and file continuing applications based on the first patent application to seek additional patents with broader patent protection than was granted on the prior patents. The scope of the claims can be slowly broadened. For example, if a significant limitation was added to the claim of the parent application to secure the patent, the applicant could allow the application to mature into a patent and simultaneously file a continuation application with similar, but broader, claims that lack the significant limitation. Filing a continuation application would therefore enable the applicant to argue for patentability of those broader claims. In this way, the patent applicant does not waste time arguing for broader patent protection in the parent application. The applicant may receive the benefit of the initial, narrower patent simply so that the invention can be marked patented, while seeking broader patent protection through the continuation application.

FAQ #24:
What types of technology should the continuation practice be applied to?

Generally, cornerstone technology

"Cornerstone technology" is technology that is incorporated across all, or most, product lines, drives most revenue sales, and/or relates to the primary benefit that the company refers to when selling its services and products. Since the continuation practice may be cost prohibitive if implemented across all product lines, I generally recommend doing so only for cornerstone technology and its peripheral technology and only if the startup has excess discretionary funds.[67]

FAQ #25:
How does the continuation practice help prevent infringement against my invention?

Maintaining patent pendency of the parent patent application

Continuation practice helps deter future competitors from entering the marketplace with the patented invention. Continuation practice allows the subject matter of the patent application to maintain pendency after the original patent is issued. Consequently, competitors would have more difficulty designing around the patent portfolio and avoid patent infringement. By filing a continuation application, the applicant can craft claims specifically directed to what competitors are attempting to use to design around the patent claims to avoid patent infringement liability. This possibility discourages potential infringers from attempting to design around the existing patent(s) in the first place. Thus, they will be less likely to enter the marketplace to compete with the patent applicant.

FAQ #26:
How much does the continuation practice cost? Does it have any other benefits?

A few thousand dollars per year, per application

Each successive continuation application eventually enters the queue for examination and incurs a cost. There are therefore repeated costs associated with filing serial continuation patent applications as well as their examinations. On average, the cost to implement a continuation practice may be a few thousand dollars per year or more. In my opinion, it is worth the cost of engaging in this practice only for cornerstone technology.

One more benefit: Improved communication with the examiner

Patent prosecution occurs in a written format, which is not conducive to clear communication. Multiple office actions and responses may need to occur for the examiner to fully appreciate the invention. Continuation practice fosters increased, dialogical correspondence and therefore helps the applicant understand the examiner's perspective of the invention and helps the examiner appreciate the full scope of patent protection that the inventor believes the invention deserves.

FAQ #27:
If I didn't file for a continuation application before my patent matured, is there any way to reinstate the patent pendency status of the original patent application?

No. But don't lose all hope!

If the patent applicant does not file a continuing application before the patent application matures into a patent, the pendency of the patent application will be terminated. However, the applicant may file a "broadening reissue patent application" (i.e., post-grant procedure) on the issued patent. The broadening reissue patent application must be filed within two years of the patent's grant date. If it is not filed within that two-year period, the claims of the issued patent cannot be broadened. Unlike a continuation application, a broadening reissue application is limited in the extent to which it can be used to broaden the claims. The broadening reissue application cannot recapture that which was given up during the original examination process. For example, if during prosecution of the patent application the patent applicant had to include a limitation narrowing the claim's scope to avoid the prior art, the applicant cannot remove the added limitation to broaden the claim via a broadening reissue application. Moreover, under the "original patent requirement," the reissue claims cannot be broadened if the subject matter of the broadened claims were merely suggested or indicated in the patent specification. They must be based on the primary invention described in the patent application.

By contrast, the claims of a continuing application may be based on a hint, suggestion, or indication and provide broad leeway in claiming aspects described in the patent application, even if those aspects are not the primary aspect of the invention. For example, a patent specification may state, "it is also contemplated that the device includes other features such as, but not limited to, X." This description may provide written description support for a claim directed to any of the X alternatives. However, the X alternatives may not be able to support the "original patent" requirement for the reissue claims if the X alternatives were repeatedly used as a feature referred to as the "invention" of the patent. The continuation patent application provides significantly more flexibility than a broadening reissue patent application for crafting the claims. Use the continuation practice for cornerstone type technology.

FAQ #28:
How can my own patent be used to reject another one of my own applications?

When it is considered prior art

An issued patent or "pre-grant publication" of a patent application can be used to reject a patent application filed later by the same entity if the patent or pre-grant publication were published more than one year before the patent application was filed. Issued patents and the pre-grant publications are prior art for patent applications filed more than one year after the publication date of the pre-grant publication or grant date of the patent. See Chapter 5 on the bars to patentability for more information.

Dealing with a double patenting rejection

It may be worth filing additional, independent patent applications or continuing applications (i.e., divisional, continuation, continuation in part, which claim priority back to the base parent application) for an auspicious invention or its improvements. However, when multiple patent applications are filed on a product with slightly different improvements, examiners may render a "double patenting rejection" if the claims in the patent applications are substantially similar.

Since multiple applications are being filed at different times and multiple patents with different termination dates may be issued, the patent owner may be able to extend the patent protection of the invention for more than the standard twenty-year term. A nonstatutory double patenting rejection would be made to prohibit the unlawful extension of patent term through the filing of multiple patent applications. However, the inventor can file a terminal disclaimer, which cuts short the patent term of any patent to make it "co-extensive" with another patent. This would avoid unlawfully extending the term of one patent in relation to other related patents. Since the doctrine of double patenting seeks to prevent the unjustified extension of patent exclusivity beyond the term of the patent, the terminal disclaimer resolves the nonstatutory double patenting rejection by cutting short the term of a later filed patent application and making it co-extensive with an earlier filed patent application.

If an examiner renders a nonstatutory double patenting rejection, the typical recommendation is to file a terminal disclaimer making the application's patent term co-extensive with the conflicting pending patent application or the issued patent. However, in some cases, such as pharmaceutical sales in which drugs may produce significant profits on a daily basis, it may be valuable to argue that a nonstatutory double patenting rejection is improper because every day the patent is extended can generate a worthwhile profit.

If, however, the examiner determines that the claims of the patent application are identical to those of the pending patent application, the rejection is a *statutory* double patenting rejection and cannot be overcome by filing a terminal disclaimer. The claims in the current, pending application may be canceled since the claimed invention has already been previously examined and issued as a patent. Additionally, if an applicant receives a statutory double patenting rejection, he or she can alternatively broaden, narrow or shift focus of the claim so that it is not identical to those of other pending, patent applications or issued patents. The statutory double patenting rejection would be changed to a nonstatutory double patenting rejection. Filing a terminal disclaimer would overcome the rejection. In this way, the applicant can broaden the claims to make them different and salvage them rather than simply canceling them.

FAQ #29:
Can I claim features and aspects invented after filing the patent application?

No!

If the new features and aspects that the inventor wants to protect were invented after the patent application was filed, they are, by definition, not included in the patent application. The claims of the patent application could not be amended and directed toward those features and aspects. If new claims are added, the examiner will render a "new matter rejection." New matter cannot be incorporated into the claims or the patent application after its filing date. The inventor should include all features and aspects in the application when the application is filed if he or she wishes to claim them.

How to avoid a new matter rejection

The new matter rejection is based on 35 U.S.C. § 132,[68] which states that no amendment shall introduce new matter into the disclosure of the invention, which often arises when claims are amended during prosecution. After the application is filed, the USPTO determines whether the substantive requirements are met and generally renders a rejection. To overcome the rejection, the claims are amended. When the claims are amended, the scope of the claims is broadened or narrowed, but the broadened or narrowed version must be supported by the patent application as filed or it will be considered new matter.

The new matter rejection is usually rendered when a limitation is added to the claims to narrow them and avoid the cited prior art. If this new limitation was not disclosed in the original patent application, the examiner will issue a new matter rejection. Arguments must be made that the new limitation is not new matter or the new limitation must be removed. Once the patent application is filed, its contents are fixed and new information (including such limitations) cannot be added to or removed. The contents of the patent application are fixed in time. The patent application should therefore include all information and peripheral aspects relevant to the point of novelty of the invention so that new limitations related to the peripheral aspects can be used to amend the claims to avoid the prior art.

Appendices

Appendix A – Trademarks

Selecting a Trademark

Under U.S. trademark laws, a trademark is anything that can identify a source of a product or service. Almost anything can serve to identify a source such as words, logos, colors, sounds, restaurant designs, product packaging, or product designs. (This is a non-exclusive list of potential types of trademarks.)

A trademark having one or more words is known as a wordmark. Examples of wordmarks include Apple, Microsoft, and General Motors. Each of these wordmarks are associated with a corresponding logo, which can also be protected by trademark rights. Other types of trademarks are more nuanced. For example, Tiffany's cyan color on its boxes, bags, and catalogs is a trademark. Microsoft trademarked its operating system's boot up sound. Coca-Cola trademarked the shape of its bottle.

However, many startups and companies do not seek protection for those more nuanced types of trademarks without good reason and funds to do so. Startups and companies more often attempt to trademark wordmarks and logos. In many cases, wordmarks are more important than logos because trademark infringement typically arises due to confusingly similar wordmarks, which is less common with logos. Moreover, consumers generally discuss products and services by referring to the wordmark and not the logo, and internet searches are usually conducted by wordmark rather than logo. The following discussion therefore focuses on how to select a trademark in terms of a wordmark.

Not all wordmarks are equally strong. Some trademarks afford less strength or breadth, whereas other wordmarks are attributed with broad protection. The strength of the trademark is dependent on its ability to be recognized as a trademark and the existence of other, similar marks already in commercial use.

Wordmarks are characterized on a scale that includes generic (not protectable), descriptive, suggestive, arbitrary, and fanciful wordmarks. The inherent quality of a mark depends on its position on this scale, which ranges from "generic" on one end, to "fanciful" on the other. "Generic wordmarks" cannot be registered or enforced against others even under common law. Examples of generic terms would be "aspirin" for a headache medicine using acetylsalicylic acid or "apple" for selling apples. "Descriptive wordmarks" describe a quality or character of the goods being sold. Descriptive wordmarks can be registered on the principal register with the United States Patent and Trademark Office as long as they are distinctive enough that consumers recognize them as a trademark rather than a descriptive term. An example of a descriptive mark is "Crystal Clear" for water. Since the law does not want to remove a competitor's ability to use these descriptive terms to describe their own goods, competitors can still use the descriptive terms in descriptive ways. For example, competitors could describe their water as "crystal clear." Suggestive, arbitrary, and fanciful marks are considered strong. The law affords broad protection for these marks since they are not very useful to competitors for marketing competing goods and services. Moreover, consumers can immediately recognize suggestive, arbitrary, and fanciful marks as inherently used as trademarks (i.e., source identifier) and not merely tools to educate the consumer of goods' qualities or characteristics.

Some companies choose to adopt marks that afford broad protection. EXXON® is a made-up word and therefore a "fanciful" mark. Apple® (computers) is an "arbitrary" mark for a term that appears in the dictionary but has no apparent link to computers or electronic devices. The law provides these marks with broad trademark protection.

EXXON® and Apple® enjoy extra protection for being famous marks. Typically, a trademark owner can assert a claim of trademark infringement against another trademark if two marks and their respective goods and/or services are similar enough that consumers would likely confuse them. Owners of famous trademarks (e.g., marks that are household names) can sue others based on dilution or weakening of a trademark's strength or unsavory association, even if there is no likelihood of confusion. In other words, even if the goods are different from each other, but the marks are similar, the law affords the famous mark a claim of trademark infringement under the "theory of dilution." For example, the "McSweet" mark for pickled cocktail onions, pickled garlic, and pickled asparagus was found to dilute the McDonald's trademark for its family of "MC" based trademarks. When selecting a trademark, be aware of where the proposed trademark lies on the generic-fanciful scale and avoid any similarity with famous trademarks.

Because online marketing is crucial for the success of most products, it is important to consider whether the trademark should correspond with an available domain name. Not all companies incorporate their trademark into their domain name. However, for those that wish to, if a domain name that corresponds with the desired trademark is not available, a different trademark should be selected.

Trademark search and application process

The trademark process has two steps. The first is a search to uncover other trademarks already used in commerce that may be similar enough to the proposed mark that likelihood of confusion would occur. Evaluating the likelihood of confusion is not an exact science. Some trademark owners may be more aggressive than others, and people's opinions differ regarding whether their trademarks are similar enough to confuse customers.

If a similar, existing trademark is found, the proposed trademark could be infringing on the rights of the existing trademark owner and should therefore be changed and a new search conducted for a different trademark. The search attempts to avoid potential trademark infringement on senior marks, which are likely to be confused with the proposed mark. It is easier to change a trademark before beginning sales. Although this process might be frustrating, businesses should undertake the search process as many times as necessary to end up with a product name that is unlikely to conflict with others.

Established businesses may have been using a trademark extensively and have built up significant goodwill around it without registering it. It would nonetheless be beneficial for those businesses to conduct a search since it could identify potential, future problems that can be addressed immediately instead of under a later threat of litigation. If a "senior mark" is identified early, a business can slowly switch to a different mark and address issues on its own timetable.

There are several types of trademark searches that are usually conducted by attorneys. Attorneys can conduct a limited search in federal and state databases for marks that are similar to the proposed mark. They can also conduct a full search for trademarks similar to the proposed mark in databases beyond federal and state, including the Internet. Obviously, the more databases one searches, the more reliable the search and opinion. I recommend clients preform preliminary clearance searches at www.uspto.gov and use the TESS database to minimize legal fees for trademark searches.

If no similar trademarks are found, the proposed mark may be properly adopted and used to brand the product or invention (given that the search is reliable). Although this clears the mark for adoption and use, it is not a guarantee that a trademark infringement lawsuit will not be asserted against the trademark owner. It does, however, reduce the likelihood of trademark infringement. As stated above, the reliability of the search-based opinion is dependent on the extent and quality of the search.

Once the search clears the mark for adoption and use, the inventor may secure trademark rights. There are three ways to establish trademark rights: (1) common law, (2) state based registration, and (3) federal based registration. There are two governmental bodies where trademark applications can be filed to register and establish ownership of trademark rights (any of the Secretary of States within the United States or at the federal level with the USPTO). There are no filing requirements to secure common law trademark rights. However, to establish protectable common law rights, the trademark owner must prove prior and sufficient use of the trademark in a geographic area where there is conflicting use, which may be difficult.

To secure state trademark rights, the trademark owner may file a trademark application with one or more states. To secure federal trademark rights, the trademark owner may file a trademark application with the USPTO. After filing the trademark application, the inventor may begin to use the mark in commerce. When the application matures into a registration, the trademark registration can be used as evidence of ownership to stop others from using a mark that is substantially similar to the registered mark. Trademark rights last until the owner abandons use of the mark or a court finds that no such rights exist.

State and federal common law trademark rights versus trademark registration

In the United States, common law rights are created whenever someone uses a mark in connection with a product or service. Trademark registration is neither required nor available for common law trademark rights. If a product is sold or a service rendered in conjunction with the mark, common law trademark or service mark rights are bestowed immediately for the benefit of the entity using that trademark or service mark. This is not the preferred means of securing trademark rights because these rights are limited to the geographical area of product sales or rendered services, with some possible geographic expansion for reputation or advertising. For example, if an entity uses a mark in Orange County but does not use the mark in commerce outside of the Orange County area, common law trademark rights are limited to the geographical area of Orange County. If the owner of the trademark is commercially successful within Orange County and plans to expand business to areas outside of the Orange County area (e.g., San Francisco), the owner must use the mark in those areas to acquire common law trademark rights there.

The problem arises when a third-party (e.g., a "good faith senior user") has already used that, or a similar, mark in a geographically remote area before the entity's expansion. The third-party is the senior user of the mark in its own geographical area and the expanding entity cannot take away the third-party's rights. Neither can the expanding entity stop innocent third-parties from using the same mark and acquiring trademark rights in a different area. These scenarios apply when no state or federal registrations are involved.

Even though common law trademark rights are established immediately upon commercial use of the mark, the owner must prove the existence of common law trademark rights to sue a third-party for trademark infringement. This is often difficult to do, and common law trademark rights are therefore not the preferred route to protect trademarks. To show ownership of common law trademark rights, the proof consists of documentary evidence showing sales, advertising, press recognition, etc., associated with the mark in all geographic areas of interest. These documents may, over a long period of time, be difficult to retrieve, making it difficult to assert common law trademark rights during litigation.

Federal and state trademark registration process

State and Federal trademark registration processes are usually simple and without the common law trademark rights' limitations. State and Federal trademark rights are established through the trademark registration process, which provides statewide or countrywide rights. Federal trademark rights are usually preferred over state trademark rights, though a state trademark registration may sometimes be necessary to sue under some state laws. Moreover, Federal trademark registration costs are not significantly more than state trademark registration costs, especially considering the national geographic scope of federal protection.

Federal trademark rights

Federal trademark rights are established when the USPTO registers the proposed mark with the principal register, establishing a "rebuttable presumption" that the registration owner has the exclusive right to use the goods or services throughout the United States. An example of a federal trademark registration is shown in Appendix D. Upon federal trademark registration, the federal trademark rights relate back to the filing date of the federal trademark application. Even if the trademark owner uses the mark in only one location, the registration establishes nationwide rights so that the trademark owner can slowly expand into new geographical regions. Furthermore, the registration gives "constructive notice" of the trademark thereby divesting third parties of any rights they may have acquired through common law.

If there is a senior user who used the mark before the filing date of the Federal trademark application, the senior user may have the right to continue using the mark only in his or her geographical region. The registration would freeze the senior user's rights to the current geographical region of use.

Federal trademark registration is an inexpensive way to demonstrate ownership of trademark rights to the mark throughout the United States in contrast to the burden of collecting and storing documents related to the use of the mark in various geographical regions to prove ownership of common law trademark rights.

State trademark rights

State trademark rights are established through a state registration process. Each state has its own registration process and trademark laws. A state trademark registration provides no enforceable rights in a different state. A state trademark application must be filed in each state in which state trademark rights are desired. It is therefore more cost effective to seek federal trademark rights if trademark rights are sought in multiple states. For a general overview of trademarks, see Chapter 3.

Appendix B – Sample Utility Patent

US007066481B1

(12) **United States Patent**
Soucek

(10) **Patent No.:** US 7,066,481 B1
(45) **Date of Patent:** Jun. 27, 2006

(54) **BICYCLE REAR SUSPENSION**

(75) Inventor: **Jeffrey A. Soucek**, Aliso Viejo, CA (US)

(73) Assignee: **Felt Racing, LLC**, Lake Forest, CA (US)

(*) Notice: Subject to any disclaimer, the term of this patent is extended or adjusted under 35 U.S.C. 154(b) by 0 days.

(21) Appl. No.: **11/104,815**

(22) Filed: **Apr. 13, 2005**

CLASS   SUBCLASS

(51) **Int. Cl.**
B62K 25/28 (2006.01)

(52) **U.S. Cl.** 280/284

(58) **Field of Classification Search** 280/283, 280/284, 285, 286; 180/227
See application file for complete search history.

(56) **References Cited**

U.S. PATENT DOCUMENTS

439,095 A	10/1890	Becker
578,615 A	3/1897	Travis
606,323 A	6/1898	Wronski
657,667 A	9/1900	Mills
944,795 A *	12/1909	Leet et al. 280/284
1,047,430 A	12/1912	Michaelson
1,257,761 A	2/1918	Strand
1,298,958 A	4/1919	Johnston
1,412,012 A	4/1922	Bruno
1,594,079 A	7/1926	Tanner
3,833,242 A	9/1974	Thompson, Jr.
3,917,313 A	11/1975	Smith et al.
3,974,892 A	8/1976	Bolger
4,322,088 A	3/1982	Miyakoshi et al.
4,506,755 A	3/1985	Tsuchida et al.
4,529,056 A	7/1985	Kreuz
4,673,053 A	6/1987	Tanaka et al.
4,789,174 A	12/1988	Lawwill
4,828,781 A	5/1989	Duplessis et al.
4,850,607 A	7/1989	Trimble

4,889,355 A	12/1989	Trimble
4,902,458 A	2/1990	Trimble
4,951,791 A	8/1990	Creixell
4,986,949 A	1/1991	Trimble
4,997,197 A	3/1991	Shultz
5,098,114 A	3/1992	Jones
5,121,937 A	6/1992	Lawwill
5,158,733 A	10/1992	Trimble
5,205,572 A	4/1993	Buell et al.
5,215,322 A	6/1993	Enders
5,244,224 A	9/1993	Busby
5,259,637 A	11/1993	Busby
5,273,303 A	12/1993	Hornzee-Jones

(Continued)

FOREIGN PATENT DOCUMENTS

DE   3033294   4/1981

(Continued)

Primary Examiner—Kevin Hurley
(74) *Attorney, Agent, or Firm*—Stetina Brunda Garred & Brucker

(57) **ABSTRACT**

A rear suspension of a bicycle may have an upper link and lower link which are pivotally connected to both a front frame and a rear frame of the bicycle such that the rear frame may rotate up and down about the front frame/front sprocket. A shock absorber may be pivotally connected to the upper link to absorb any impact forces imposed on the rear wheel and transferred to the upper link as the rear frame rotates up and down. Also, the upper link may be interconnected to the lower link with a tie link which allows the upper and lower links to work in conjunction with each other such that pedal setback is negligible when the rear wheel rides over bumps along the bike trail. Additionally, the tie link equalizes the forces caused by the rider's weight and pedaling forces.

10 Claims, 3 Drawing Sheets

US 7,066,481 B1

Page 2

U.S. PATENT DOCUMENTS

5,306,036 A	4/1994	Busby	
5,335,929 A	8/1994	Takagaki et al.	
5,354,085 A	10/1994	Gally	
5,368,804 A	11/1994	Hwang et al.	
5,409,249 A	4/1995	Busby	
5,441,292 A	8/1995	Busby	
5,456,481 A	10/1995	Allsop et al.	
D372,002 S	7/1996	Busby et al.	
6,036,211 A *	3/2000	Nohr	280/276
6,036,213 A	3/2000	Busby	
2005/0067806 A1*	3/2005	Weagle	280/124.1
2005/0067810 A1*	3/2005	Wengle	280/284

FOREIGN PATENT DOCUMENTS

GB	15332	0/1915
GB	220760	6/1923
GB	2167361 A *	5/1986
IT	428442	12/1947
JP	5105168	4/1993
WO	WO 9215477	8/1992
WO	WO 9313974	7/1993

* cited by examiner

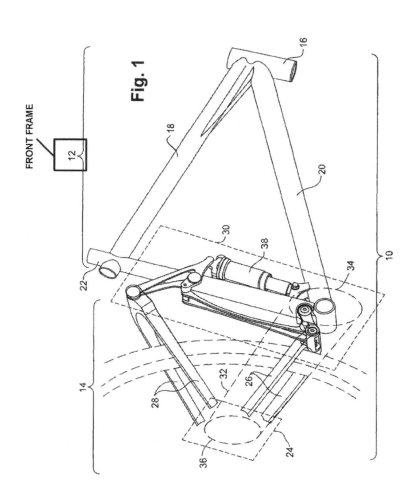

Fig. 1

FRONT FRAME

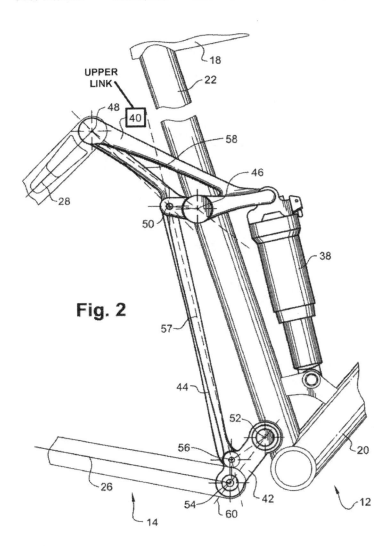

UPPER
LINK

Fig. 2

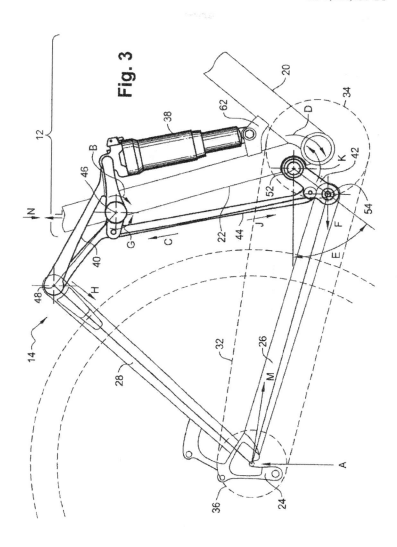

Fig. 3

US 7,066,481 B1

<table>
<tr><td>

1

BICYCLE REAR SUSPENSION

BACKGROUND OF THE INVENTION

The present invention relates to a bicycle rear suspension system.

Mountain bikes are designed to be ridden over dirt trails. These dirt trails may have gravel, dirt, leaves, uneven terrain (e.g., boulders) and other elements which cause vibration and sudden jolts in the pedals, handlebar and seat of the bike. The vibration and jolts cause the bike rider to become fatigued at a faster rate compared to the fatigue rate if the rider had been riding over a smooth surface. For example, a mountain bike ridden over gravel causes vibration in the handlebar and seat. The rider must compensate for the vibration by absorbing the vibration with his/her arms and legs. As such, the rider must use additional energy to ride his/her bike over gravel. In another example, a mountain bike ridden over a mountain trail may have obstacles (e.g., boulders) that the rider must maneuver over or around. These obstacles or boulders may suddenly impact the bike's front and rear tires which are transferred to the bike's pedals, seat and handlebar. The rider must also absorb these impact forces with his/her legs and arms. Prolonged and repeated exposure to these sudden impact forces causes the rider to become fatigued at a faster rate compared to the fatigue rate if the rider had been riding over a smooth surface.

Modern mountain bikes are currently designed to reduce the amount of vibration and any impact forces transferred to the pedals, handlebar and seat. For example, mountain bikes may be installed with front shocks. The front shocks help to absorb any impact forces to the front tire and vibration caused by gravel, dirt, leaves, and obstacles on the bike trail. Similarly, mountain bikes may be fabricated with rear wheel suspension systems. These suspension systems help to absorb any vibration and sudden impact forces to the rear wheel caused by gravel, dirt, leaves, and obstacles on the bike trail. One typical rear wheel suspension system is a four bar linkage. The four bar linkage permits the rear wheel to rotate clockwise and counter clockwise about the front sprocket when the rear wheel rides over gravel, dirt, leaves, and obstacles along the bike trail. The four bar linkage is also connected to a shock absorber to absorb the impact forces caused by the terrain of the bike trail. In this way, the rear suspension system provides a smoother and more comfortable ride to the user.

Unfortunately, rear suspension systems such as the four bar linkage cause pedal setback when the rear wheel travels over the uneven terrain of the bike trail. The reason is that the rear wheel does not travel along a circular path about the front sprocket. Rather, the distance between the rear wheel (i.e., rear sprocket) and the front sprocket increases and decreases as the rear wheel is rotated about the front sprocket to absorb the impact forces caused by gravel, dirt, and obstacles along the bike trail. As such, the rider must compensate for the pedal setback causing the rider to become fatigued at a faster rate than if the rider was riding over a smooth surface. In sum, although rear suspension systems of bicycles help to reduce vibration and impact shocks by absorbing them into a shock absorber, rear suspension systems still have other inherent problems such as pedal setback.

Accordingly, there is a need in the art for an improved bicycle rear suspension that exhibits negligible or no pedal setback.

</td><td>

2

BRIEF SUMMARY OF THE INVENTION

The present invention addresses the above-described deficiencies as well as other deficiencies associated with the prior art. In an aspect of the present invention, a rear suspension is provided which is disposed between a front frame and a rear frame of the bicycle. In particular, the suspension system may comprise an upper link which is pivotably connected to both the front frame (i.e., at the seat tube) and the rear frame at a front upper pivot point and a rear upper pivot point, respectively. Also, a shock absorber may be pivotally connected to the upper link opposite from the rear upper pivot point with respect to the seat tube. This creates a lever by which the shock absorber can absorb any impact shocks received through the rear wheel and rear frame.

The suspension system may also comprise a lower link pivotally connected to the front frame and the rear frame at a front lower pivot point and a rear lower pivot point, respectively. The lower link maintains a constant distance between the rear wheel/rear sprocket and the front sprocket as the suspension system absorbs impact forces (i.e., as the rear wheel travels up and down). As such, the rider only experiences a negligible amount of pedal setback.

This is achieved by interconnecting the lower link to the upper link via a tie link. The lower link, the upper link and the tie link which interconnects the lower link and the upper link regulate the path of the rear sprocket as the rear wheel rides over the uneven terrain of the bike trail and as the rear frame is re-stabilized. In particular, when the rear wheel rides over the uneven terrain, the rear sprocket rotates about the front sprocket. Since the rear sprocket/rear wheel is also connected to the upper link and a shock absorber, any shocks are absorbed into the shock absorber. However, the rear wheel moves closer to the front frame due to the rotation of the upper link. To counteract the forward movement of the rear sprocket, the upper link is also connected to the tie link and the lower link. The tie link applies a corresponding force on the lower link when the rear wheel is rotated about the front sprocket. Since the lower link is initially angled downwardly, the rotation of the lower link moves the rear wheel/rear sprocket away from the front sprocket. Accordingly, the upper link which moves the rear wheel closer to the front sprocket is balanced by the lower link which moves the rear wheel away from the front sprocket, and vice versa. Hence, negligible pedal setback occurs as the suspension system absorbs impact shocks and restabilizes.

Also, the tie link applies equalizing forces to the lower link and the upper link to stabilize the forces imposed on the rear frame due to pedal forces and the rider's weight. In particular, the rider's weight exerts an upward force on the tie link due to the clockwise rotation of the upper link and the lower link when the rider sits on the bike seat. In contrast, the pedaling forces exert a downward force on the tie link due to the counterclockwise rotation of the upper link and the lower link when the rider pedals. These upward and downward forces are equalized through the tie link so as to provide the rider with a smoother ride and negligible pedal setback.

BRIEF DESCRIPTION OF THE DRAWINGS

These as well as other features of the present invention will become more apparent upon reference to the drawings wherein:

FIG. 1 is a rear perspective view of a front frame connected to a suspension system of a rear frame;

</td></tr>
</table>

US 7,066,481 B1

3

FIG. 2 is a front plane view of the suspension system; and

FIG. 3 is a front plane view of the rear frame and suspension system.

DETAILED DESCRIPTION OF THE INVENTION

The drawings refe[...] he purposes of illustrating the vario[...] t invention and are not meant [...] sent invention. R[...] to FIG. 1, a bicycle 10 is shown having a front frame 12 and rear frame 14. The front frame 12 has a head tube 16, a top tube 18, a down tube 20 and a seat tube 22. The head tube 16 contains a head set which provides the interface with the bicycle forks, front tire and handle bar. The top tube 18 connects the head tube 16 to the seat tube 22 at the top, and the down tube 20 connects the head tube 16 to the seat tube 22 at the bottom. Accordingly, the front frame 12 may have a triangular configuration. However, it is also contemplated within the scope of the present invention that the various aspects of the present invention may be employed with a front frame 12 having a configuration other than a triangular configuration.

The rear frame 14 is connected to the rear dropouts 24 (see FIGS. 1 and 3), where the rear wheel is rotateably connected. The rear dropouts 24 are more clearly shown in FIG. 3 and disposed on opposed sides of the rear wheel. The rear frame 14 has a pair of chain stays 26 and a pair of suspension stays 28. The chain stays 26 connect a suspension system 30 of the bicycle 10 to the rear dropouts 24 and run parallel to a chain 32 on opposed sides of the rear wheel. The suspension stays 28 run diagonally downward on opposed sides of the rear wheel also connecting the suspension system 30 of the bicycle 10 to the rear dropouts 24. Accordingly, as shown in FIG. 1, the rear frame 14 is independent from the front frame 12 in that they 12, 14 are not directly connected to each other 12, 14 but are connected to each other 12, 14 via the suspension system 30. This provides for a bicycle 10 which exhibits negligible pedal setback when the rear wheel rides over bumps (e.g., boulders) along the bike trail. As such, the power generated by the rider is efficiently transferred through the crank to the rear wheel.

The suspension system 30 is disposed between the front frame 12 and rear frame 14. The suspension system 30 is pivotably attached to both the front frame 12 and the rear frame 14 and absorbs any impact forces when the rear wheel rides over bumps along the bike trail. For example, as the rider rides along the bike trail, the front wheel may go over a bump along the bike trail. The impact force of the bump on the front wheel may be absorbed by front shocks. The bump may then impact the rear wheel pushing the rear wheel and the rear frame 14 in a generally upward direction. However, since the rear wheel and rear frame 14 are independent from the front frame 12, the impact force from the bump is transferred into a shock absorber 38 of the suspension system 30. Hence, the rider does not feel the impact of the bump on the rear wheel as much as if the rider had been riding a hardtail bike.

The suspension system 30 of the present invention also creates a negligible amount of pedal setback caused by the impact force of the bump on the rear wheel. Pedal setback may be caused by chain growth/reduction between the front sprocket 34 and the rear sprocket 36 as the rear wheel rides over bumps along the bike trail. For example, in prior art suspension systems, the rear wheel and the rear frame are generally pushed upward when the bike's rear wheel

4

impacts a bump. The rear wheel which is also connected to the rear sprocket does not maintain the same distance to the front sprocket as the rear wheel is pushed upward. Since the front sprocket and rear sprocket are connected to each other via a chain, any changes in distance from the front sprocket to the rear sprocket [...] ance or retract (i.e., pedal setback). T[...] r retraction of the pedal must be abs[...] present invention, pedal setback is r[...] daling force of the rider is more efficiently transferred to the rear wheel compared to prior art bikes with a rear suspension system.

Referring now to FIG. 2, the suspension system 30 may comprise an upper link 40, lower link 42, tie link 44, and the shock absorber 38 which are pivotably connected to each other as well as the front and rear frames 12, 14 to provide for a bicycle suspension system 30 which reduces the amount of pedal setback compared to prior art suspension systems. The upper link 40 is pivotably connected to the front frame 12 at a front upper pivot point 46, the rear frame 14 at a rear upper pivot point 48 and the tie link 44 at a top pivot point 50. The lower link 42 is also pivotably connected to the front frame 14 at a front lower pivot point 52, the rear frame 14 at a rear lower pivot point 54 and the tie link 44 at a bottom pivot point 56. The shock absorber 38 may be connected to the upper link 40 to absorb energy transferred to the rear frame 14 when the rear wheel rides over a bump along the trail.

The upper link 40 is connected to the front frame 12, rear frame 14 and the tie link 44 at the front upper pivot point 46, rear upper pivot point 48 and the top pivot point 50, respectively. These points 46, 48, 50 as shown in FIG. 2 have a triangular configuration. Also, the lower link 42 is connected to the front frame 12, rear frame 14 and tie link 44 at the front lower pivot point 52, rear lower pivot point 54 and the bottom pivot point 56, respectively. These points 52, 54, 56 as shown in FIG. 2 also have a triangular configuration. The upper link and the lower link may be pivotably connected to each other through the tie link 44. The tie link 44 defines the direction of forces exerted on the upper link 40 and the lower link 42 by the tie link 44. The direction of the forces is along a tie link line 57 which extend between the front and rear upper pivots points 46, 48 of the upper link 40 and the front and rear lower pivot points 52, 54 of the lower link 42. The relationships assist in maintaining the distance between the rear wheel/rear sprocket 36 and the front sprocket 34 such that the rider experiences negligible to no pedal setback.

Furthermore, the front upper pivot point 46 and the rear upper pivot point 48 may define an upper base line 58 extending through these points 46, 48, and the front lower pivot point 52 and the rear lower pivot point 54 may define a lower base line 60 extending through these points 52, 54. The top pivot point 50 may be located under the upper base line 58 and disposed between the upper base line 58 and the lower base line 60. Similarly, the bottom pivot point 56 may be located above the lower base line 60 and disposed between the lower base line 60 and the upper base line 58. These relationships between the pivot points 46, 48, 50, 52, 54, 56 assist the rear sprocket 36 (see FIG. 1) to substantially maintain its distance to the front sprocket 34 (see FIG. 1) when the rear wheel and rear frame 14 are pushed upwardly by a bump along the bike trail path. As such, the rider experiences negligible pedal setback as the rider rides over bumps along the bike trail path. Also, the shock absorber 38 is connected to the upper link 40 and designed to absorb the impact energy transferred into the rear frame 14 when the bump impacts the rear wheel.

5

Referring now to FIG. 3, the distance between the front sprocket **34** and the rear sprocket **36** may be substantially maintained throughout the upward and downward travel of the rear wheel when a bump along the bike trail path impacts the rear wheel. In particular, when the bump impacts the rear wheel, the rear frame **14** is quickly pushed upwardly in the direction of arrow A causing the upper link **40** to rotate clockwise in the direction of arrow B about the front upper pivot point **46**. The rear upper pivot point **48** rotates clockwise about the front upper pivot point **46** thereby traversing the rear sprocket **36** closer to the front frame **12** in the horizontal direction. Since the shock absorber **38** is located opposite to the front upper pivot point **46**, the shock absorber **38** absorbs the impact force of the bump. Additionally, the tie link **44** is also pushed upwardly in the direction of arrow C causing the lower link **42** to rotate in a clockwise direction in the direction of arrow D about the front lower pivot point **52**. The lower link **42** is initially positioned at a negative angle E in relation to the horizontal plane. As such, when the lower link **42** is rotated in clockwise direction D, the rear lower pivot point **54** is traversed away from the front frame **12** in the direction F. The traversal of the rear sprocket closer to the front frame **12** and of the rear lower link pivot point **54** away from the front frame **12** substantially maintains the distance between the front sprocket **34** and the rear sprocket **36** such that there is no chain growth therebetween **34**, **36** and the rider experiences only a negligible amount of pedal setback.

After the impact force of the bump has been absorbed by the shock absorber **38**, the shock absorber **38** rotates the upper link **40** in a counter-clockwise direction G pushing the rear upper link pivot point **48** downwards and away in the direction H from the front frame **12**. This downward motion traverses the rear sprocket away from the front frame **12**. Additionally, the counter clockwise rotation of the upper link **40** pushes the tie link **44** downward in direction J as well ....

rota~~ ~~

whic ~~c) an upper link pivotably attached to the front frame at a~~
fram ~~front upper pivot point and the rear frame at a rear~~ frame **12**. This traverses the rear sprocket **36** closer to the front sprocket **12**. The traversal of the rear upper pivot point **48** away from the front frame **12** and the rear lower pivot point **54** closer to the front frame **12** maintains the distance between the front sprocket **34** and the rear sprocket **36** such that the rider experiences only a negligible amount of pedal set back. As such, the suspension system **30** efficiently transfers the pedal power generated by the rider through the crack and into the rear wheel to propel the rider and bike along the bike trail effortlessly as the suspension system **30** absorbs the impact force of the bump and re-stabilizes.

The suspension system **30** also equalizes the pedal forces generated by the rider and the rider's weight. The pedal forces generated by the rider during pedaling generally cause the seat of the bike **10** to rise upwardly in direction L. The reason is that chain **32** attempts to pull the rear sprocket **36** forward in direction M when the rider is pedaling thus causing a counter clockwise rotation in direction K of the lower link **42** about the front lower pivot point **52** and a downward force on the tie link **44** causing the rear wheel to push down on the bike trail. In contrast, the rider's weight pushes down on the bike's seat in direction N causing the upper link **40** to rotate in a clockwise rotation in direction B about the front upper pivot point **46** and exert an upward force on the tie link **44**. Accordingly, the tie link equalizes the upward force imposed on the tie link **44** by the rider's weight and the downward force imposed on the tie link **44** by the pedal forces.

6

The suspension system **30** may also be improved by fabricating the rear frame **14**, and more particularly, the chain stays **26** and/or the suspension stays **28** from carbon fiber to allow the rear frame **14** to flex as the rear frame **14** is pushed upwardly and downwardly. This allows the rear frame **14** to absorb shocks in addition to the shock absorber **38**. For example, when the rear wheel rides over a bump, the rear frame **14** may bend slightly to absorb the impact of the bump. Additionally, the carbon fiber allows the rear frame **14** to compensate for any imbalance between the rotations of the upper link **40** and the lower link **42**.

The shock absorber **38** may be attached to the upper link **40**. The attachment point is on the opposite side of the rear upper pivot point **48**. This provides a lever mechanism such that the energy causing the upward movement of the rear frame **14** is transferred into the absorber **38**. By way of example and not limitation, the shock absorber **38** may be a gas shock. The shock absorber **38** may also be adjustable by pumping the shock absorber with additional air or releasing air from the pressure chamber of the shock absorber **38**. The shock absorber **38** may also be connected to the front frame **12**, and more particularly, to the front frame **12** at a junction defined by the seat tube **22** and the down tube **20**. As shown in FIG. 3, the shock absorber is connected to a bracket **62** welded to the junction of the seat tube **22** and the down tube **20**.

The upper link **40**, lower link **42**, tie link **44**, rear frame **14**, front frame **12**, and the shock absorber **38** are all pivotably connected to each other. These pivotal connections may be accomplished with ball bearings to provide minimal friction between the respective parts to allow the most efficient transfer of energy into the shock absorber.

Additional modifications and improvements of the present invention may also be apparent to those of ordinary skill in the art. Thus, the particular combination of parts and steps described and illustrated herein are intended to represent ...~~ain~~ embodiments of the present invention, and ...~~d~~ to serve as limitations of alternative devices ...~~within~~ the spirit and scope of the invention.

What is claimed is:

A suspension system comprising:

a) a front frame;

b) a rear frame;

c) an upper link pivotably attached to the front frame at a
front upper pivot point and the rear frame at a rear
upper pivot point, the front and rear upper pivot points
defining an upper base line;

d) a lower link pivotably attached to the front frame at a
front lower pivot point, the front and rear lower pivot
points defining a lower base line; and

e) a tie link pivotably attached to the upper link at a top
pivot point and the lower link at a bottom pivot point,
the top and bottom pivot points disposed between the
upper base line and the lower base line.

2. The system of claim 1 wherein the rear upper pivot
point, the front upper pivot point and the top pivot point
forms a triangle.

3. The system of claim 2 wherein the rear lower pivot
point, the front lower pivot point and the bottom pivot point
forms a triangle.

4. The system of claim 3 wherein forces acting on the top
pivot point and the bottom pivot point are directed toward
each other.

5. The system of claim 1 wherein the rear frame has a V
shaped configuration.

US 7,066,481 B1

7

6. The system of claim **1** wherein the rear frame is fabricated from carbon fiber.

7. The system of claim **1** further comprising a shock absorber pivotally connected to the upper link and the front frame to absorb any impact forces imposed on a rear wheel of a bicycle.

8. The system of claim **1** wherein the front frame is independently connected to the rear frame via the upper and lower links.

9. A suspension system comprising:

a) a front frame;

b) a rear frame;

c) an upper link pivotably attached to the front frame at a front upper pivot point and the rear frame at a rear upper pivot point;

8

d) a lower link pivotably attached to the front frame at a front lower pivot point and the rear frame at a rear lower pivot point; and

e) a tie link pivotably attached to the upper link at a top pivot point and the lower link at a bottom pivot point;

f) wherein a tie link line defined by the top and bottom pivot points extend between the front and rear upper pivot points of the upper link and the front and rear upper pivot points of the lower link.

10. The system of claim **9** wherein the front and rear upper pivot points define an upper base line, the front and rear lower pivot points define a lower base line, and the top and bottom pivot points are disposed between the upper base line and the lower base line.

* * * * *

Appendix C – Sample Design Patent

US00D761364S

(12) **United States Design Patent**
    Summerville, Jr.

(10) **Patent No.:**   **US D761,364 S**
(45) **Date of Patent:**   **   **Jul. 12, 2016**

(54) **CHESSBOARD**

(71) Applicant: **SUMMERVILLE-NEW ENGLAND LLC**, Goshen, CT (US)

(72) Inventor: **Andrew Goodwin Summerville, Jr.,** Goshen, CT (US)

(73) Assignee: **SUMMERVILLE-NEW ENGLAND LLC**, Goshen, CT (US)

(**) Term: **14 Years**

(21) Appl. No.: **29/500,023**

(22) Filed: **Aug. 20, 2014**

(51) **LOC (10) Cl.** **21-01**

(52) **U.S. Cl.**
    USPC D21/397; D21/349

(58) **Field of Classification Search**
    USPC D21/348, 362–371, 307, 302, 308–309,
      D21/306, 334, 335–341, 345–347, 349,
      D21/374–377, 300, 390, 397, 455, 458, 459,
      D21/478, 480, 519, 522, 811, 812, 350;
      273/260, 261, 236–244, 348, 394, 258,
      273/259, 274–277, 268–271, 280–287, 278,
      273/279, 288–291, 138.1, 139, 141 R,
      273/141 A, 142 R, 143 R, 143 A, 143 B,
      273/143 C, 142 E, 142 F, 142 G, 142 H,
      273/142 HA, 145 E, 294, 292, 298, 148 R,
      273/309, 153 R, 155, 156, 157 R, 153 J, 161,
      273/440, 459–461, 317, 340, 342, 108,
      273/126 R, 126 A, 127 R, 348.1, 348.3,
      273/348.4, 348.5, 351, 355, 367, 373, 374,
      273/393, 403–412, 248, 249; 473/14, 10,
      473/16; 272/280, 284, 309; 108/167, 119,
      108/62; D6/691, 691.1
    CPC A63F 3/00; A63F 3/00003; A63F 3/02;
      A63F 3/04; A63F 3/00082; A63F 3/00088;
      A63F 3/00091; A63F 3/00097; A63F 3/00173;
      A63F 3/00176; A63F 3/0023; A63F 3/0052;
      A63F 3/00694; A63F 3/027; A63F 3/062;
      A63F 3/0625; A63F 2003/00022; A63F
      2003/00208; A63F 2003/00463; A63F

      2003/0047; A63F 2003/00523; A63F
      2009/0033; A63F 2009/0035; A63F
      2009/0047; A63F 9/0073; A63F 3/00895;
      A63F 2003/00287; A63F 2003/00987; A63F
      2003/00968; A63F 2003/00977; A63F
      2003/00949; A63D 15/04

See application file for complete search history.

(56)   **References Cited**

          U.S. PATENT DOCUMENTS

16,116	A	*	11/1856	Goodwin A63F 3/0023 273/284
25,529	A	*	9/1859	Sargent A63F 3/0023 273/284
28,733	A	*	6/1860	Brooks A63F 3/0023 273/284
107,065	A	*	9/1870	Kmth .... A63F 3/0023 273/157 R
118,249	A	*	8/1871	Kintz .... A63F 3/0023 273/142 E
139,425	A	*	5/1873	Schindler A63F 3/00895 108/62
150,735	A	*	5/1874	Whitcomb A63F 3/00895 273/287
161,502	A	*	3/1875	Gilbert A47B 13/08 108/90
163,630	A	*	5/1875	Bourn A63F 3/0023 273/284
164,654	A	*	6/1875	Moulton A63F 3/0023 273/284
166,776	A	*	8/1875	Herzog .... A63F 3/0023 273/148 R
175,495	A	*	3/1876	Pottin A63D 15/04 108/33
178,267	A	*	6/1876	Buckley et al. A63F 3/0023 273/284
178,268	A	*	6/1876	Buckley A63F 3/0023 273/284
186,181	A	*	1/1877	Underwood A63F 3/0023 273/260
250,458	A	*	12/1881	Shay A63F 3/0023 273/284
344,062	A	*	6/1886	Sterges A63F 3/0023 273/284
352,555	A	*	11/1886	Merkel A63F 3/0023 108/119
359,820	A	*	3/1887	Seliger A63F 3/0023 273/284

US D761,364 S
Page 2

527,279	A	*	10/1894	Green	A63F 3/0023	273/284
538,380	A	*	4/1895	McKenzie	A63F 3/0023	273/286
571,464	A	*	11/1896	Truex	A63F 3/02	273/258
573,972	A	*	12/1896	Hamilton	A63F 3/0023	273/284
574,192	A	*	12/1896	Climenson	A63F 3/02	235/90
577,984	A	*	3/1897	Horovitz	A63F 3/00895	273/280
D27,788	S	*	10/1897	Haskell		273/284
613,550	A	*	11/1898	Ballou	A63F 3/02	273/260
621,799	A	*	3/1899	Degges	A63F 3/02	273/260
636,663	A	*	11/1899	Harrison	A63F 3/00895	273/151
687,487	A	*	11/1901	Powell	A63F 3/0695	273/281
689,137	A	*	12/1901	Snyder	A63F 3/02	273/260
695,431	A	*	3/1902	Atwood	A63F 3/02	273/260
715,794	A	*	12/1902	Haskell	A63F 3/0023	273/284
716,435	A	*	12/1902	Lackner	A63F 3/00895	273/287
718,147	A	*	1/1903	Nientimp	A63F 3/0023	273/284
724,760	A	*	4/1903	Van Altena	A63F 3/0023	273/286
734,092	A	*	7/1903	Read	A63F 3/0023	174/40 TD
801,903	A	*	10/1905	Paxton	A63F 3/02	273/260
817,233	A	*	4/1906	Emmerling	A63F 3/02	273/146
841,366	A	*	1/1907	Yorke	A63F 3/0023	273/283
847,655	A	*	3/1907	Davidson	A63F 3/0023	273/284
895,875	A	*	8/1908	Mercer	A63F 3/0023	273/260
1,030,521	A	*	6/1912	Maxim	A63F 3/02	273/260
1,044,309	A	*	11/1912	Waldo	A63F 3/0023	273/284
1,092,599	A	*	4/1914	Schilling	A63F 3/0023	273/261
1,106,052	A	*	8/1914	Newell	A63F 3/0023	273/284
1,119,870	A	*	12/1914	Pettit	A63F 3/00574	273/282.1
1,262,821	A	*	4/1918	Marks	A63F 3/0023	273/282.1
1,348,262	A	*	8/1920	Brockway	A63H 3/52	108/11
1,400,520	A	*	12/1921	Bugenhagen	A63F 3/02	273/260
1,412,314	A	*	4/1922	Pandolfo	A47B 3/02	108/119
1,418,409	A	*	6/1922	Wakefield	A63F 3/0023	273/260
1,421,678	A	*	7/1922	Ebert	A63F 3/02	273/258
1,510,853	A	*	10/1924	Latz	A63F 3/00697	273/288
1,532,069	A	*	3/1925	Ortiz	A63F 3/0023	273/148 R
1,535,503	A	*	4/1925	Spaeder	A63F 3/0023	273/285
1,553,655	A	*	9/1925	Wadel	A63F 3/0023	273/285
1,596,918	A	*	8/1926	Brunner	A63F 3/0023	273/242
1,621,185	A	*	3/1927	Bain	A63F 3/02	273/284
1,641,104	A	*	8/1927	Solod	A63F 3/0023	273/285
1,850,420	A	*	3/1932	Schuldt	A63F 1/06	108/13
1,877,154	A	*	9/1932	Weaver	A63F 3/00075	273/241
1,928,790	A	*	10/1933	Luhn	A63F 1/06	273/284
2,066,244	A	*	12/1936	Bates	A63F 3/02	273/260
2,075,619	A	*	3/1937	Klemin	A63F 3/00574	273/241
2,196,861	A	*	4/1940	Gruber	A63F 3/00697	273/282.1
D137,786	S	*	4/1944	Paige	D21/349	
2,420,482	A	*	5/1947	Janik	A63F 3/0023	273/260
2,424,123	A	*	7/1947	Schruben	A63F 3/0023	273/285
D167,382	S	*	7/1952	Wales	D21/335	
2,665,913	A	*	1/1954	Hlavac	A63F 3/00694	235/90
3,018,107	A	*	1/1962	Erickson	A63F 3/02	273/237
3,163,425	A	*	12/1964	Caplan	A63F 3/02	273/260
D204,277	S	*	4/1966	Neal		273/285
D210,542	S	*	3/1968	Stookey		273/241
3,380,402	A	*	4/1968	Simpson	A47B 13/16	108/25
3,520,537	A	*	7/1970	Peebles	A63F 3/00697	273/282.1
3,529,372	A	*	9/1970	Kutsch	A47F 7/146	273/282.1
3,532,342	A	*	10/1970	Grays	A63F 3/0023	273/260
3,602,514	A	*	8/1971	Peebles	A63F 3/00697	273/116
D222,890	S	*	1/1972	White	D7/605	
3,741,547	A	*	6/1973	Zurek	A63F 3/00895	273/239
3,751,039	A	*	8/1973	Dykoski	A63F 3/00697	273/241
D228,775	S	*	10/1973	Randell		273/260
3,792,186	A	*	2/1974	Principe	G09B 19/22	273/287
3,794,326	A	*	2/1974	Bialek	A63F 3/00895	273/146
D231,542	S	*	4/1974	Munson, Jr.		273/287
3,802,708	A	*	4/1974	Libert	A63F 3/00643	108/23
3,804,418	A	*	4/1974	Sander	A63F 3/00261	273/260
3,871,657	A	*	3/1975	Lorenz	A63F 3/0214	273/239
3,908,999	A	*	9/1975	Brown	A63F 3/00697	273/146
4,003,535	A	*	1/1977	Tianchon	A47B 13/04	248/188
4,015,778	A	*	4/1977	Chen	A47C 4/24	273/260
4,019,746	A	*	4/1977	Hare	A63F 3/00697	273/260
4,043,559	A	*	8/1977	Eigen	A63F 3/0457	273/236
4,065,125	A	*	12/1977	Chan	A47B 25/00	473/14
4,099,723	A	*	7/1978	Robinson	A63F 3/02	273/241
D252,047	S	*	6/1979	Citrone	D21/349	
4,188,035	A	*	2/1980	Metzler, Jr.	A63F 3/00697	273/260
4,312,507	A	*	1/1982	Smith	A47B 23/001	108/23
4,326,720	A	*	4/1982	Erlich	A63F 3/00697	273/239
4,371,168	A	*	2/1983	Dupuis	A63F 3/0023	206/315.1
D287,146	S	*	12/1986	Lin		273/286

US D761,364 S

Page 3

4,673,184 A	*	6/1987	Sansores	A63F 3/0023 273/286
D292,353 S	*	10/1987	Chien	D6/686
4,708,349 A	*	11/1987	Shomer	A63F 3/02 273/261
D296,909 S		7/1988	Lin	D21/335
4,781,384 A	*	11/1988	Bois	A63F 3/0023 206/1.5
4,856,789 A	*	8/1989	Carlson	A63F 3/02 273/261
4,967,925 A	*	11/1990	Feniello	A63F 3/00895 220/524
4,984,808 A	*	1/1991	Young	A63F 3/00697 206/315.1
5,040,800 A	*	8/1991	Ulau	A63F 3/00574 273/239
D328,476 S		8/1992	Titus	D21/336
D330,805 S	*	11/1992	Yang	A63F 3/02 273/287
5,160,145 A	*	11/1992	Bokhagen	A63F 3/02 273/260
5,171,018 A	*	12/1992	Zhang	A63F 3/0415 273/260
D343,204 S	*	1/1994	Schramer	D21/349
5,275,414 A	*	1/1994	Stephens	A63F 3/02 273/261
5,280,913 A	*	1/1994	Sirk	A63F 3/0023 206/311
5,306,017 A	*	4/1994	Huston	A63F 3/02 273/261
5,314,189 A	*	5/1994	Kerivan	A63F 3/00697 273/260
D349,521 S		8/1994	Harris, III et al.	
5,338,041 A	*	8/1994	Jones	A63F 3/02 273/259
5,356,155 A	*	10/1994	Gross	A63F 3/00895 273/284
5,358,252 A		10/1994	McPhaul	
D360,234 S	*	7/1995	Knight	D21/349
D363,091 S		10/1995	Dobis	
D366,190 S	*	1/1996	Vance	D21/348
5,513,849 A	*	5/1996	Navin	A63F 3/00176 273/261
D371,166 S		6/1996	Furlong	
5,556,099 A	*	9/1996	Mardirosian	A63F 3/00214 273/241
D374,688 S		10/1996	Furlong	
5,577,730 A	*	11/1996	Vannozzi, Sr.	A63F 3/0023 206/315.1
5,662,326 A	*	9/1997	Gebran	A63F 3/00694 273/239
5,749,583 A	*	5/1998	Sadounichvili	A63F 3/02 273/260
5,779,239 A	*	7/1998	Lind	A63F 3/02 273/243
D405,127 S	*	2/1999	Bao	D21/349
5,865,436 A	*	2/1999	Conti	A63F 3/00031 273/241
5,954,333 A	*	9/1999	Vilches Guerra	A63F 3/02 273/261
6,102,399 A	*	8/2000	Kifer	A63F 3/00176 273/261
6,113,182 A	*	9/2000	Wise	A47B 85/06 108/13
6,116,602 A	*	9/2000	McLoy	A63F 3/00176 273/260
D434,456 S		11/2000	Bracken	
6,142,474 A	*	11/2000	Tachkov	A63F 3/02 273/260
D437,360 S		2/2001	Golling	D21/335
D448,054 S		9/2001	Dominguez	D21/341
6,412,778 B1		7/2002	Alaimo	
6,478,300 B1	*	11/2002	Pickett	A63F 3/00697 273/258
D467,282 S		12/2002	Glover	D21/337
6,595,143 B2	*	7/2003	London	A47D 3/00 108/25
6,662,732 B2	*	12/2003	Birsel	A47B 21/00 108/25
D490,254 S	*	5/2004	Stanton	D6/691.3

D500,529 S	*	1/2005	Mauser	D21/338
6,902,165 B1	*	6/2005	Hunt	A63F 3/02 273/236
D513,139 S	*	12/2005	Bibi	D6/691.1
6,976,434 B2	*	12/2005	Roig	A47B 25/00 108/25
D513,908 S	*	1/2006	Bibi	D6/691.1
D513,909 S	*	1/2006	Bibi	D6/691.1
D526,027 S		8/2006	Smith	
D526,497 S	*	8/2006	Snell	D6/358
D533,737 S	*	12/2006	Bibi	D21/397
D534,377 S	*	1/2007	Bibi	D21/397
D534,378 S	*	1/2007	Bibi	D21/397
D534,743 S	*	1/2007	Bibi	D21/397
D534,744 S	*	1/2007	Bibi	D21/397
D540,070 S	*	4/2007	Bibi	D21/397
D540,071 S	*	4/2007	Bibi	D21/397
D540,569 S	*	4/2007	Bibi	D21/397
D540,570 S	*	4/2007	Bibi	D21/397
D551,469 S	*	9/2007	Bibi	D21/397
7,273,212 B1	*	9/2007	Kolbaba	A47B 11/00 108/103
D554,197 S	*	10/2007	Henschel	D21/338
D555,401 S	*	11/2007	Adams	D6/691.1
D555,942 S	*	11/2007	Adams	D21/397
D565,328 S	*	4/2008	Lowsky	D6/691.1
D577,227 S	*	9/2008	Brooks	D6/691
D577,526 S	*	9/2008	Lowsky	D6/707.18
D654,960 S	*	2/2012	Bruzzaniti	D21/397
D655,469 S	*	3/2012	Millar	D32/40
D688,750 S	*	8/2013	Douglas	D21/336
8,833,769 B1	*	9/2014	Hilvitz	A63F 3/0023 273/283
D740,373 S	*	10/2015	Martin	D21/397
2004/0150160 A1	*	8/2004	Giegerich	A63F 3/0023 273/287
2005/0077678 A1	*	4/2005	Bibi	A63F 3/00895 273/28
2006/0232007 A1	*	10/2006	Kuehn	A63F 3/0023 273/239
2007/0102881 A1	*	5/2007	Holden	A63F 3/0023 273/260
2009/0014956 A1	*	1/2009	Sutor, Jr.	A63F 3/0023 273/286
2009/0058003 A1	*	3/2009	Nouhan, Jr.	A63F 3/02 273/260
2010/0102510 A1	*	4/2010	Stapleford	A63F 3/0023 273/285
2015/0014930 A1	*	1/2015	Summerville, Jr.	A63F 3/00261 273/260

* cited by examiner

Primary Examiner — Susan Moon Lee

(74) *Attorney, Agent, or Firm* — Stetina Brunda Garred & Brucker

(57)   **CLAIM**

The ornamental design for a chessboard, as shown and described.

FIRST EMBODIMENT

DESCRIPTION

FIG. 1 is a perspective view of a first embodiment of a chessboard, shown integrated into a table;

FIG. 2 is a top view of the chessboard and table shown in FIG. 1;

FIG. 3 is a front view of the chessboard and table shown in FIG. 1;

FIG. 4 is a rear view of the chessboard and table shown in FIG. 1;

FIG. 5 is a left view of the chessboard and table shown in FIG. 1;

FIG. 6 is a right view of the chessboard and table shown in FIG. 1;

SECOND EMBODIMENT   **US D761,364 S**

Page 4

FIG. 7 is a bottom view of the chessboard and table shown in FIG. 1;

FIG. 8 is a front cross-sectional view of the chessboard and table as shown in FIG. 2;

FIG. 9 is a left cross-sectional view of the chessboard and table shown in FIG. 2;

FIG. 10 is a perspective view of a second embodiment of the chessboard, shown integrated into a table;

FIG. 11 is a top view of the chessboard and table shown in FIG. 11;

FIG. 12 is a front view of the chessboard and table shown in FIG. 11;

FIG. 13 is a rear view of the chessboard and table shown in FIG. 11;

FIG. 14 is a left view of the chessboard and table shown in FIG. 11;

FIG. 15 is a right view of the chessboard and table shown in FIG. 11;

FIG. 16 is a bottom view of the chessboard and table shown in FIG. 11;

FIG. 17 is a front cross-sectional view of the chessboard and table shown in FIG. 11;

FIG. 18 is a left cross-sectional view of the chessboard and table shown FIG. 11.

Broken lines and unshaded portions contained within broken lines depict portions of the chessboard and of a table that are environmentally illustrative and form no part of the claimed design.

1 Claim, 12 Drawing Sheets

FIG. 1

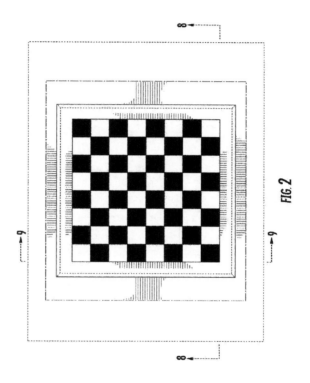

FIG. 2

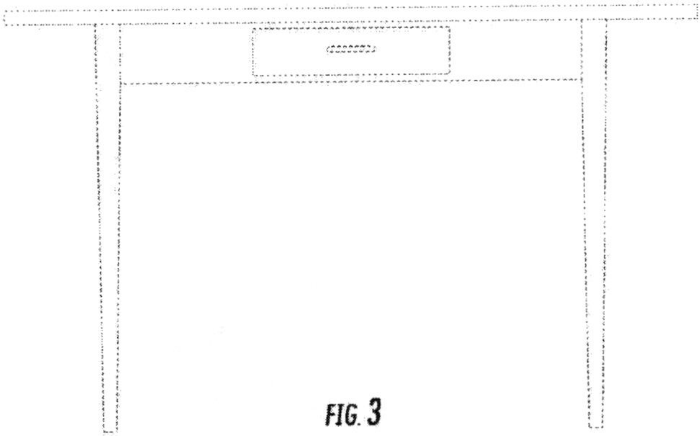

FIG. **3**

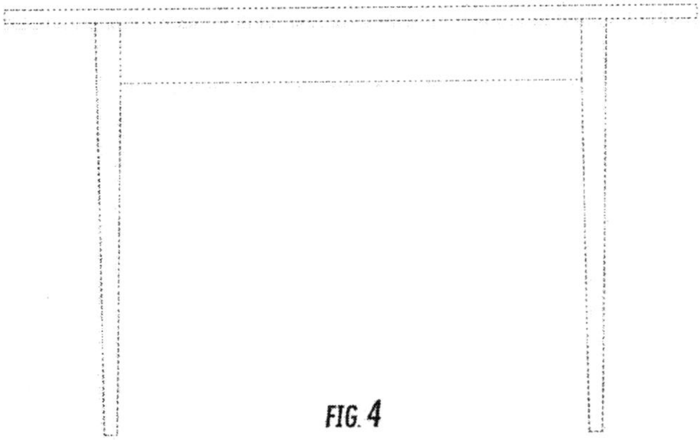

FIG. **4**

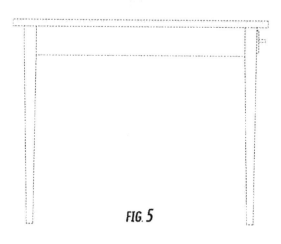

FIG. **5**

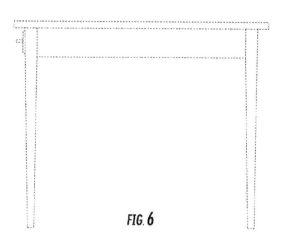

FIG. **6**

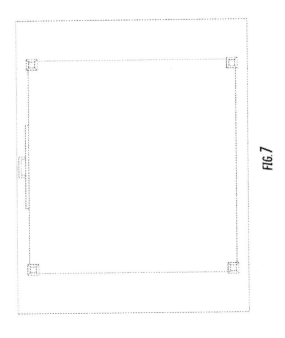

FIG. 7

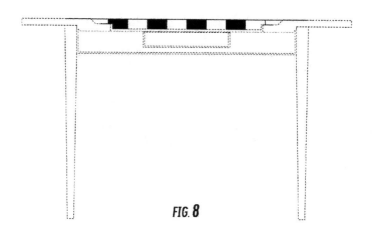

FIG. **8**

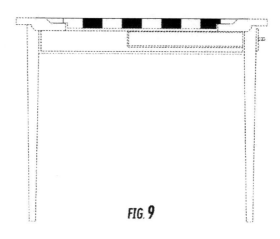

FIG. **9**

FIG. 10

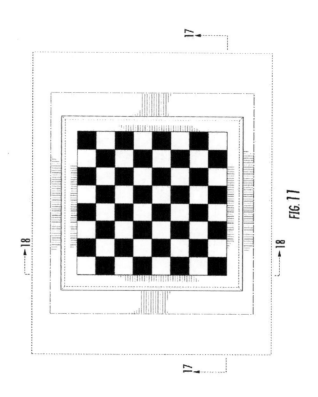

FIG. 11

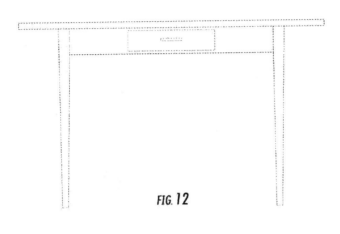

FIG. 12

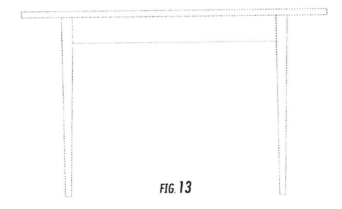

FIG. 13

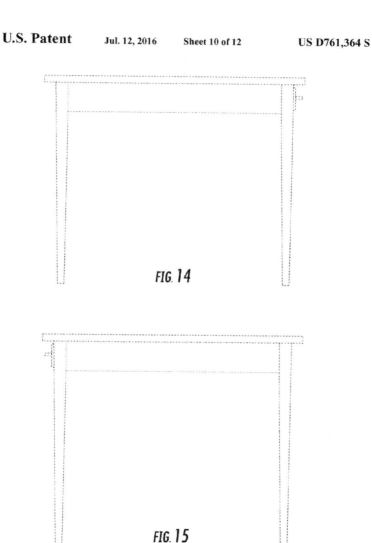

FIG. 14

FIG. 15

FIG. 16

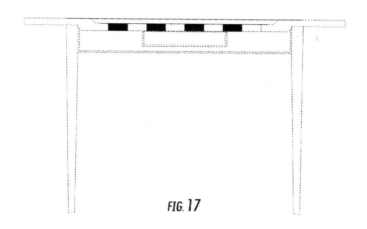

FIG. 17

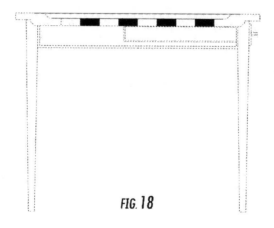

FIG. 18

Appendix D - Sample Trademark Registration

United States of America
United States Patent and Trademark Office

WHOLESALE NUTRITION CENTER

Reg. No. 4,805,669
Registered Sep. 1, 2015
Int. Cl.: 35

SERVICE MARK
SUPPLEMENTAL REGISTER

BETTER BODY CONSULTING, INC. (CALIFORNIA CORPORATION)
446 W. 19TH ST.
COSTA MESA, CA 92627

FOR: RETAIL STORE SERVICES FEATURING SPORTS NUTRITIONAL PRODUCTS, WEIGHT LOSS PRODUCTS, VITAMINS, WEIGHT GAINERS, AMINO ACIDS, CREATINE, PROTEIN DRINKS, AND PROTEIN BARS, IN CLASS 35 (U.S. CLS. 100, 101 AND 102).

FIRST USE 10-11-2010; IN COMMERCE 10-11-2010.

THE MARK CONSISTS OF STANDARD CHARACTERS WITHOUT CLAIM TO ANY PARTICULAR FONT, STYLE, SIZE, OR COLOR.

NO CLAIM IS MADE TO THE EXCLUSIVE RIGHT TO USE "WHOLESALE", APART FROM THE MARK AS SHOWN.

SER. NO. 86-407,760, FILED P.R. 9-26-2014; AM. S.R. 7-15-2015.

MAYUR VAGHANI, EXAMINING ATTORNEY

Director of the United States
Patent and Trademark Office

Appendix E – Entity Size

Large entity, small entity or micro-entity status

The US Patent and Trademark Office (USPTO) has a three tiered fee structure. The first tier is referred to as a large entity. By default, an applicant is a large entity and must pay large entity fees. The second tier is referred to as a small entity. The small entity pays a reduced fee of about 50% the fee compared to the large entity. The third tier is referred to as a micro-entity. The micro-entity pays a reduced fee of about 75% the fee compared to the large entity.

Small entity:

A small entity is defined as:
1. An independent inventor;
2. A small business; **or**
3. A non profit organization (e.g., university, 501(c)(3)).
Also, small entity status is lost if any patent rights are assigned or licensed to an entity that is a large entity.

A small business is defined as an entity with 500 or fewer employees within the past year including part time employees. If your company is close to the 500 employee mark, the recommendation would be to pay the large entity fee to be on the safe side. Otherwise, validity of any patent maturing from the patent application may be in jeopardy.

Small entity status is lost and large entity fees paid only when the issue fee or maintenance fee are being paid.

Micro-Entity:

A micro-entity is an entity that would qualify as a small entity plus the entity must:
Must not have been named as an inventor on more than

4 previously filed patent applications; Must not have, in the calendar year preceding the calendar year in which the applicable fee is paid, have a gross income exceeding 3 times the median household income; and Must not have assigned, granted or conveyed (and is not under an obligation to do so) a license or other ownership interest in the application concerned to an entity that, in the calendar year preceding the calendar year in which the applicable fee is paid, had a gross income exceeding 3 times the median household income.

As of 2017, three times the median household income is $169,548/year. If the inventor's stated income levels is close to this amount, the recommendation would be file as a small entity to be on the safe side. Otherwise, validity of any patent maturing from the patent application may be in jeopardy.

When applying the micro-entity definition, applicants are not considered to be named on a previously-filed application if he/she has assigned, or is obligated to assign, ownership rights as a result of previous employment. The definition includes applicants who are employed by an institute of higher education (as defined in 20 U.S.C. 1001(a)) and have assigned, or are obligated to assign ownership to that institute of higher education.

Also, micro-entity status is lost and small entity fees paid as soon as the above criteria are not met.

Appendix F - Patent Laws

35 U.S.C. 100 (note) America Invents Act (AIA) First inventor to file provisions.

The first inventor to file provisions of the Leahy-Smith America Invents Act (AIA) apply to any application for patent, and to any patent issuing thereon, that contains or contained at any time—

(A) a claim to a claimed invention that has an effective filing date on or after March 16, 2013 wherein the effective filing date is:

(i) if subparagraph(ii) does not apply, the actual filing date of the patent or the application for the patent containing a claim to the invention; or

(ii) the filing date of the earliest application for which the patent or application is entitled, as to such invention, to a right of priority under section 119, 365(a), 365(b), 386(a), or 386(b) or to the benefit of an earlier filing date under section 120, 121, 365(c), or 386(c); or

(B) a specific reference under section 120, 121, 365(c), or 386(c) of title 35, United States Code, to any patent or application that contains or contained at any time such a claim.

35 U.S.C. 100 Definitions.

[Editor Note: 35 U.S.C. 100(e)-(j) as set forth below are only applicable to patent applications and patents subject to the first inventor to file provisions of the AIA (35 U.S.C. 100 (note)). See 35 U.S.C. 100(e) (pre-AIA) for subsection (e) as otherwise applicable.]

When used in this title unless the context otherwise indicates—

(a) The term "invention" means invention or discovery.

(b) The term "process" means process, art, or method, and includes a new use of a known process, machine, manufacture, composition of matter, or material.

(c) The terms "United States" and "this country" mean the United States of America, its territories and possessions.

(d) The word "patentee" includes not only the patentee to whom the patent was issued but also the successors in title to the patentee.

(e) The term "third-party requester" means a person requesting ex parte reexamination under section 302 who is not the patent owner.

(f) The term "inventor" means the individual or, if a joint invention, the individuals collectively who invented or discovered the subject matter of the invention.

(g) The terms "joint inventor" and "coinventor" mean any 1 of the individuals who invented or discovered the subject matter of a joint invention.

(h) The term "joint research agreement" means a written contract, grant, or cooperative agreement entered into by 2 or more persons or entities for the performance of experimental, developmental, or research work in the field of the claimed invention.

(i)

(1) The term "effective filing date" for a claimed invention in a patent or application for patent means—

(A) if subparagraph (B) does not apply, the actual

filing date of the patent or the application for the patent containing a claim to the invention; or

(B) the filing date of the earliest application for which the patent or application is entitled, as to such invention, to a right of priority under section 119, 365(a), 365(b), 386(a), or 386(b) or to the benefit of an earlier filing date under section 120, 121, 365(c), or 386(c).

(2) The effective filing date for a claimed invention in an application for reissue or reissued patent shall be determined by deeming the claim to the invention to have been contained in the patent for which reissue was sought.

(j) The term "claimed invention" means the subject matter defined by a claim in a patent or an application for a patent.

35 U.S.C. 101 (AIA and Pre-AIA) Inventions patentable.

Whoever invents or discovers any new and useful process, machine, manufacture, or composition of matter, or any new and useful improvement thereof, may obtain a patent therefor, subject to the conditions and requirements of this title.

35 U.S.C. 102 (AIA) Conditions for patentability; novelty.

[Editor Note: Applicable to any patent application subject to the first inventor to file provisions of the AIA (see 35 U.S.C. 100 (note)). See 35 102 (pre-AIA) for the law otherwise applicable.]

(a) NOVELTY; PRIOR ART.—A person shall be entitled to a patent unless—

(1) the claimed invention was patented, described in

a printed publication, or in public use, on sale, or otherwise available to the public before the effective filing date of the claimed invention; or

(2) the claimed invention was described in a patent issued under section 151, or in an application for patent published or deemed published under section 122(b), in which the patent or application, as the case may be, names another inventor and was effectively filed before the effective filing date of the claimed invention.

(b) EXCEPTIONS.—

(1) DISCLOSURES MADE 1 YEAR OR LESS BEFORE THE EFFECTIVE FILING DATE OF THE CLAIMED INVENTION.—A disclosure made 1 year or less before the effective filing date of a claimed invention shall not be prior art to the claimed invention under subsection (a)(1) if—

(A) the disclosure was made by the inventor or joint inventor or by another who obtained the subject matter disclosed directly or indirectly from the inventor or a joint inventor; or

(B) the subject matter disclosed had, before such disclosure, been publicly disclosed by the inventor or a joint inventor or another who obtained the subject matter disclosed directly or indirectly from the inventor or a joint inventor.

(2) DISCLOSURES APPEARING IN APPLICATIONS AND PATENTS.—A disclosure shall not be prior art to a claimed invention under subsection (a)(2) if—

(A) the subject matter disclosed was obtained directly or indirectly from the inventor or a joint inventor;

(B) the subject matter disclosed had, before such subject matter was effectively filed under subsection (a)(2), been publicly disclosed by the inventor or a joint inventor or another who obtained the subject matter disclosed directly or indirectly from the inventor or a joint inventor; or

(C) the subject matter disclosed and the claimed invention, not later than the effective filing date of the claimed invention, were owned by the same person or subject to an obligation of assignment to the same person.

(c) COMMON OWNERSHIP UNDER JOINT RESEARCH AGREEMENTS.—Subject matter disclosed and a claimed invention shall be deemed to have been owned by the same person or subject to an obligation of assignment to the same person in applying the provisions of subsection (b)(2)(C) if—

(1) the subject matter disclosed was developed and the claimed invention was made by, or on behalf of, 1 or more parties to a joint research agreement that was in effect on or before the effective filing date of the claimed invention;

(2) the claimed invention was made as a result of activities undertaken within the scope of the joint research agreement; and

(3) the application for patent for the claimed invention discloses or is amended to disclose the names of the parties to the joint research agreement.

(d) PATENTS AND PUBLISHED APPLICATIONS EFFECTIVE AS PRIOR ART.—For purposes of determining whether a patent or application for patent is prior art to a claimed invention under subsection (a)(2), such patent or application shall be considered to have been effectively filed, with respect to any subject matter described in the patent or application—

(1) if paragraph (2) does not apply, as of the actual filing date of the patent or the application for patent; or

(2) if the patent or application for patent is entitled to claim a right of priority under section 119, 365(a), 365(b), 386(a), or 386(b), or to claim the benefit of an earlier filing date under section 120, 121, 365(c), or 386(c) based upon 1 or more prior filed applications for patent, as of the filing date of the earliest such application that describes the subject matter.

*NOTE: The provisions of 35 U.S.C. 102(g), as in effect on **March 15, 2013**, shall also apply to each claim of an application for patent, and any patent issued thereon, for which the first inventor to file provisions of the AIA apply (see 35 U.S.C. 100 (note)), if such application or patent contains or contained at any time a claim to a claimed invention to which is **not** subject to the first inventor to file provisions of the AIA.]

35 U.S.C. 102 (pre-AIA) Conditions for patentability; novelty and loss of right to patent.

[Editor Note: With the exception of subsection (g)*), not applicable to any patent application subject to the first inventor to file provisions of the AIA (see 35 U.S.C. 100 (note)). See 35 U.S.C. 102 for the law otherwise applicable.]

A person shall be entitled to a patent unless—

(a) the invention was known or used by others in this country, or patented or described in a printed publication in this or a foreign country, before the invention thereof by the applicant for patent, or

(b) the invention was patented or described in a printed publication in this or a foreign country or in public use or on sale in this country, more than one year prior to the date of the application for patent in the United States, or

(c) he has abandoned the invention, or

(d) the invention was first patented or caused to be patented, or was the subject of an inventor's certificate, by the applicant or his legal representatives or assigns in a foreign country prior to the date of the application for patent in this country on an application for patent or inventor's certificate filed more than twelve months before the filing of the application in the United States, or

(e) the invention was described in — (1) an application for patent, published under section 122(b), by another filed in the United States before the invention by the applicant for patent or (2) a patent granted on an application for patent by another filed in the United States before the invention by the applicant for patent, except that an international application filed under the treaty defined in section 351(a) shall have the effects for the purposes of this subsection of an application filed in the United States only if the international application designated the United States and was published under Article 21(2) of such treaty in the English language; or

(f) he did not himself invent the subject matter sought to be patented, or

(g) (1) during the course of an interference conducted under section135 or section 291, another inventor involved therein establishes, to the extent permitted in section 104, that before such person's invention thereof the invention was made by such other inventor and not abandoned, suppressed, or concealed, or (2) before such person's invention thereof, the invention was made in this country by another inventor who had not abandoned, suppressed, or concealed it. In determining priority of invention under this subsection, there shall be considered not only the respective dates of conception and reduction to practice of the invention, but also the reasonable diligence of one who was first to conceive and last to reduce to practice, from a time prior to conception by the other.

*NOTE: The provisions of 35 U.S.C. 102(g), as in effect on March 15, 2013, shall apply to each claim of an application for patent, and any patent issued thereon, for which the first inventor to file provisions of the AIA apply (see 35 U.S.C. 100 (note), if such application or patent contains or contained at any time—

(A) a claim to an invention having an effective filing date as defined in section 100(i) of title 35, United States Code, that occurs before March 16, 2013; or

(B) a specific reference under section 120, 121, or 365(c) of title 35, United States Code, to any patent or application that contains or contained at any time such a claim.

35 U.S.C. 103 (AIA) Conditions for patentability; non-obvious subject matter.

[Editor Note: Applicable to any patent application subject to the first inventor to file provisions of the AIA (see 35 U.S.C. 100 (note)). See 35 U.S.C. 103 (pre-AIA) for the law otherwise applicable.]

A patent for a claimed invention may not be obtained, notwithstanding that the claimed invention is not identically disclosed as set forth in section 102, if the differences between the claimed invention and the prior art are such that the claimed invention as a whole would have been obvious before the effective filing date of the claimed invention to a person having ordinary skill in the art to which the claimed invention pertains. Patentability shall not be negated by the manner in which the invention was made.

35 U.S.C. 103 (pre-AIA) Conditions for patentability; non-obvious subject matter.

[Editor Note: Not applicable to any patent application subject to the first inventor to file provisions of the AIA (see 35 U.S.C. 100 (note)). See 35 U.S.C. 103 for the law otherwise applicable.]

(a) A patent may not be obtained though the invention is not identically disclosed or described as set forth in section 102, if the differences between the subject matter sought to be patented and the prior art are such that the subject matter as a whole would have been obvious at the time the invention was made to a person having ordinary skill in the art to which said subject matter pertains. Patentability shall not be negatived by the manner in which the invention was made.

(b)

(1) Notwithstanding subsection (a), and upon timely election by the applicant for patent to proceed under this subsection, a biotechnological process using or resulting in a composition of matter that is novel under section 102 and nonobvious under subsection (a) of this section shall be considered nonobvious if- (A) claims to the process and the composition of matter are contained in either the same application for patent or in separate applications having the same effective filing date; and (B) the composition of matter, and the process at the time it was invented, were owned by the same person or subject to an obligation of assignment to the same person.

(2) A patent issued on a process under paragraph (1)-(A) shall also contain the claims to the composition of matter used in or made by that process, or (B) shall, if such composition of matter is claimed in another patent, be set to expire on the same date as such other patent, notwithstanding

section 154.

(3) For purposes of paragraph (1), the term "biotechnological process" means- (A) a process of genetically altering or otherwise inducing a single- or multi-celled organism to- (i) express an exogenous nucleotide sequence, (ii) inhibit, eliminate, augment, or alter expression of an endogenous nucleotide sequence, or (iii) express a specific physiological characteristic not naturally associated with said organism; (B) cell fusion procedures yielding a cell line that expresses a specific protein, such as a monoclonal antibody; and (C) a method of using a product produced by a process defined by subparagraph (A) or (B), or a combination of subparagraphs (A) and (B).

(c)

(1) Subject matter developed by another person, which qualifies as prior art only under one or more of subsections (e), (f), and (g) of section 102, shall not preclude patentability under this section where the subject matter and the claimed invention were, at the time the claimed invention was made, owned by the same person or subject to an obligation of assignment to the same person.

(2) For purposes of this subsection, subject matter developed by another person and a claimed invention shall be deemed to have been owned by the same person or subject to an obligation of assignment to the same person if—

(A) the claimed invention was made by or on behalf of parties to a joint research agreement that was in effect on or before the date the claimed invention was made;

(B) the claimed invention was made as a result of activities undertaken within the scope of the joint research agreement; and

(C) the application for patent for the claimed invention discloses or is amended to disclose the names of the parties to the joint research agreement.

(3) For purposes of paragraph (2), the term "joint research agreement" means a written contract, grant, or cooperative agreement entered into by two or more persons or entities for the performance of experimental, developmental, or research work in the field of the claimed invention.

35 U.S.C. 112 (AIA) Specification.

[Editor Note: Applicable to any patent application filed on or after September 16, 2012. See 35 U.S.C. 112 (pre-AIA) for the law otherwise applicable.]

(a) IN GENERAL.—The specification shall contain a writtendescription of the invention, and of the manner and process of making and using it, in such full, clear, concise, and exact terms as to enable any person skilled in the art to which it pertains, or with which it is most nearly connected, to make and use the same, and shall set forth the best mode contemplated by the inventor or joint inventor of carrying out the invention.

(b) CONCLUSION.—The specification shall conclude with one or more claims particularly pointing out and distinctly claiming the subject matter which the inventor or a joint inventor regards as the invention.

(c) FORM.—A claim may be written in independent or, if the nature of the case admits, in dependent or multiple dependent form.

(d) REFERENCE IN DEPENDENT FORMS.—Subject to subsection (e), a claim in dependent form shall contain a reference to a claim previously set forth and then specify a further limitation of the subject matter claimed. A claim in dependent form shall be construed to incorporate by reference all the limitations of the claim to which it refers.

(e) REFERENCE IN MULTIPLE DEPENDENT FORM.—A claim in multiple dependent form shall contain a reference, in the alternative only, to more than one claim previously set forth and then specify a further limitation of the subject matter claimed. A multiple dependent claim shall not serve as a basis for any other multiple dependent claim. A multiple dependent claim shall be construed to incorporate by reference all the limitations of the particular claim in relation to which it is being considered.

(f) ELEMENT IN CLAIM FOR A COMBINATION.—An element in a claim for a combination may be expressed as a means or step for performing a specified function without the recital of structure, material, or acts in support thereof, and such claim shall be construed to cover the corresponding structure, material, or acts described in the specification and equivalents thereof.

35 U.S.C. 112 (pre-AIA) Specification.

[Editor Note: Not applicable to any patent application filed on or after September 16, 2012. See 35 U.S.C. 112 for the law otherwise applicable.]

The specification shall contain a written description of the invention, and of the manner and process of making and using it, in such full, clear, concise, and exact terms as to enable any person skilled in the art to which it pertains, or with which it is most nearly connected, to make and use the same, and shall set forth the best mode contemplated by the inventor of carrying out his invention.

The specification shall conclude with one or more claims particularly pointing out and distinctly claiming the subject matter which the applicant regards as his invention.

A claim may be written in independent or, if the nature of the case admits, in dependent or multiple dependent form.

Subject to the following paragraph, a claim in dependent form shall contain a reference to a claim previously set forth and then specify a further limitation of the subject matter claimed. A claim in dependent form shall be construed to incorporate by reference all the limitations of the claim to which it refers.

A claim in multiple dependent form shall contain a reference, in the alternative only, to more than one claim previously set forth and then specify a further limitation of the subject matter claimed. A multiple dependent claim shall not serve as a basis for any other multiple dependent claim. A multiple dependent claim shall be construed to incorporate by reference all the limitations of the particular claim in relation to which it is being considered.

An element in a claim for a combination may be expressed as a means or step for performing a specified function without the recital of structure, material, or acts in support thereof, and such claim shall be construed to cover the corresponding structure, material, or acts described in the specification and equivalents thereof.

35 U.S.C. 132 (AIA and Pre-AIA) Notice of rejection; reexamination.

(a) Whenever, on examination, any claim for a patent is rejected, or any objection or requirement made, the Director shall notify the applicant thereof, stating the reasons for such rejection, or objection or requirement, together with such information and references as may be useful in judging of the propriety of continuing the prosecution of his application; and if after receiving such notice, the applicant persists in his claim for a patent, with or without amendment, the application shall be reexamined. <u>No amendment shall introduce new matter into the disclosure of the invention.</u>

(b) The Director shall prescribe regulations to provide for the continued examination of applications for patent at the request of the applicant. The Director may establish appropriate fees for such continued examination and shall provide a 50 percent reduction in such fees for small entities that qualify for reduced fees under section 41(h) (1).

*NOTE: Emphasis added.

Endnotes

1   To be precise, this is not a monopolistic right because the inventor's patent right is not a "positive right" to make, use, sell, offer for sale the patented invention in the United States or import the patented invention into the United States. Rather, the patent right is stated as a "negative right," an exclusionary right that can be asserted against others to stop the enumerated activities listed above.

2   Even though it is crucial to construct the "specification" (i.e., written explanation of how to make and use the invention) around the point of novelty, the focus of the claim should also be on the point of novelty. However, the focus of the claims and the specification on the point of novelty should not be fixed in stone. During examination, there might be a reason to shift the focus of the claims away from the originally identified point of novelty. For example, the examiner may cite (i.e., find and point to) a prior art reference that includes or discloses the identified point of novelty for which the inventor is seeking patent protection. There may be prior art that includes the mechanical clicker system mentioned above. If this is the case, then the claims of the new patent application should be focused on a more refined aspect of mechanical clicker system or on a secondary feature (e.g., grip or removable eraser). For more about the intricacies of how claims are constructed, please see Chapter 11.

3   For an example of class and subclass categorizations, see Appendix B describing a patent I obtained for a client who invented a rear suspension for a mountain bicycle. This patent is categorized in class 280 which, refers to land vehicles, and subclass 284, which refers to rear suspensions.

4   Third-party prior art search companies include WASHPAT LLC (www.washpat. com) and Clarivate Analytics (http://ip.thomsonreuters.com/product/patent-search-services).

5   "Reasonable" steps differ based on the value of the trade secret—the more potentially valuable the information, the more steps must be taken to secure its secrecy. For example, reasonable steps to maintain the secrecy of the Coca-Cola formula would be higher than reasonable steps to maintain the secrecy of the customer list of a local injection molding company. Reasonable steps for the local injection molding company might include requesting all persons that have access to its customer list to enter into a confidentiality agreement. By contrast, to safeguard the Coca- Cola formula with only a confidentiality agreement may not be sufficiently reasonable. Because the value of the Coca-Cola formula is great, reasonable efforts would likely include the confidentiality agreement in addition to other steps including, but not limited to, dividing out manufacturing steps so that

no one plant manufactures the Coca-Cola drink.

6   For inventions directed to a plant patent, I recommend seeking advice of a patent attorney specializing in plant patent since that is outside my area of competence.

7   New *Railhead Mfg., L.L.C. v. Vermeer Mfg. CO.*, 298 F.3d 1290 (2002).

8   *Hamilton Beach Brands, Inc. v. Sunbeam Prods., Inc.*, 726 F.3d 1370 (Fed. Cir. 2013).

9   *Topliff v. Topliff*, 145 U.S. 156 (1982).

10   The design patent application contains a specification and drawings. The specification contains a simple statement claiming "a design as shown in the drawings" and a generic description of the various drawings. The generic description of the drawings is a simple labeling of the views that are shown. An example of this section can be seen in the example design patent application in Appendix C. This section only deals with the drawings.

11   *Arc'Teryx Equip, Inc. v. Westcomb Outerwear, Inc.*, 2:07-cv-59 (D. Utah Nov. 4, 2008).

12   The "minimally competitive alternative product" refers to the bare-bones essence of the invention and how it works. It may also be described as the invention's point of novelty or the point of departure from what is already known in the prior art or existing technology.

13   The Claims Section is a difficult and sometimes time-consuming to prepare and requires an experienced attorney to prepare competently. For example, a full Claim Set may include (1) claims directed to the apparatus and method of use and (2) claims directed to different entities that the inventor would like to stop should those competitors decide to make, use, offer for sale, sell, or import their invention into the United States. Drafting a Claims Set in a way that offers the optimal possible protection for the inventor is an incredibly nuanced process. The Claim Set may also have to take into consideration the business and marketing environment in addition to the invention itself. For more about the Claims, see Chapter 11.

14   Aspects of the invention unrelated to the point of novelty are generally not included in the patent application, but aspects that intersect with the point of novelty should be included. Competent patent counsel should be consulted to determine which alternative embodiments and peripheral features should be included in the patent application. Alternative embodiments achieve the same results as the invention but a different or sub-optimal way. Peripheral features describe, for example, the types of materials used to make the invention.

15   The enablement requirement is dictated by statute 35 U.S.C. § 112(a), which states "the specification shall contain a written description of the invention, and of the manner and process of making and using it, in such full, clear, concise, and exact terms as to enable any person skilled in the art to which it pertains, or with

which it is most nearly connected, to make and use the same, and shall set forth the best mode contemplated by the inventor or joint inventor of carrying out the invention." (See also Appendix F).

16   See Appendix F "The sole purpose of the best mode requirement is to restrain inventors from applying for patents while at the same time concealing from the public preferred embodiments of their inventions, which they have in fact conceived. The best mode inquiry focuses on the inventor's state of mind at the time he filed his application, raising a subjective factual question. The specificity of disclosure required to comply with the best mode requirement must be determined by the knowledge of facts within the possession of the inventor at the time of filing the application." See *Glaxo, Inc. v. Novopharm* LTD., 52 F3d 1043, 1050 (Fed. Cir. 1995). The enablement requirement can be distinguished from the best mode requirement as: "Enablement looks to placing the subject matter of the claims generally in the possession of the public. Best mode looks to whether specific instrumentalities and techniques have been developed by the inventor and known to him at the time of filing as the best way of carrying out the invention. The enablement requirement, thus, looks to the objective knowledge of one of ordinary skill in the art, while the best mode inquiry is a subjective, factual one, looking to the state of the mind of the inventor." *Glaxo, Inc. v. Novopharm* LTD., 52 F.3d 1043, 1050 (Fed. Cir. 1995).

17   *Gentry Gallery, Inc. v. Berkline Corp.*, 134 F.3d 1473, 45 USPQ2d 1498 (Fed. Cir. 1998). 35 U.S.C. § 112 sets forth the requirement for the specification of the patent application by requiring that it contain a written description of the invention in sufficient detail to enable a person of ordinary skill in the art to practice the claimed invention. See Appendix F.

18   *Crown Packaging v. Ball Metal* (Fed. Cir. 2011).

19   The patent at issue had broad claims directed to one, but not both, of the features. The claims were broadly written, referencing only the large angle chuck wall (Figure 6, #24) regardless of the width of the reinforcing bead (Figure 6, #25). In *Crown packaging v. Ball Metal*, the defendant (Ball Metal) argued that Crown Packaging's patent *claim* did not satisfy the "written description requirement," as the *specification* did not describe in the embodiment that was directed only to the large angle chuck wall (Figure 6, #24). Instead, the specification referenced both the large angle of the chuck wall (Figure 6, #24) and the narrow reinforcing bead (Figure 8, #25). The District Court agreed with the alleged infringer but on appeal and after reviewing the specification and the structure of the application's Claim Set, the Federal Circuit reversed this decision and the patent owner won. Regarding the specification, the Federal Circuit stated: "nowhere does the specification teach that metal saving can only be achieved by increasing the chuck wall angle *along with* narrowing the reinforcing bead" (emphasis mine). With respect to the structure of the claim, the Federal circuit noted that the original independent claims were directed to the chuck wall angle without reference to the narrow reinforcing bead and that the narrow reinforcing bead limitation was added as a dependent claim. The claims show that the applicant's conception of the invention was limited to

reducing the metal used only with a large angle chuck wall, regardless of the size of the reinforcing bead. Hence, according to the Federal Circuit's decision, the written description requirement was met.

20   *Revolution Eyewear, Inc. v. Aspex Eyewear*, 90 USPQ 1733 (Fed. Cir. 2009).

21   In a case title, the patent owner is usually listed first and the accused patent infringer second. However, the accused patent infringer is listed first if a patent owner has threatened litigation against an accused patent infringer who then counter-files a "declaratory judgement action" (DJ action). An accused patent infringer requests a DJ action to declare that there is no infringement. This enables the accused patent infringer to continue to conduct business without being under the threat of litigation. With a DJ action, an accused patent infringer does not have to wait for the patent owner to file the patent infringement lawsuit. This is what happened in this case.

22   Revolution (the accused infringer) had built a similar device but mounted the sunglass lenses on the bottom, instead of the top, of the magnetized projections on the lenses. Revolution argued that the patent owner's patent claims of infringement were invalid for not being commensurate with the scope of the detailed description. The patent specification discussed both the decreased strength and stable support problems of the prior art and asserted that the claimed invention solved these two problems. However, the claims were directed to only the decreased strength problem and not the stable support problem. Since the claims were broad enough to cover both top and bottom mounted sunglass lenses, Revolution contended that the claims were not commensurate with the detailed description. The Court disagreed. It held that inventors can craft claims to address one problem or several and that the written description requirement is satisfied as to each claim as long as the description conveys that the inventor was in possession of the invention recited in the claims.

23   During litigation, courts interpret the terms and phrases used in the claims based on intrinsic and extrinsic evidence. Intrinsic evidence includes words used to describe the invention in the patent application and the Background Section. Intrinsic evidence also includes the correspondence between the patent applicant and the USPTO. Extrinsic evidence includes dictionary definitions, expert opinion, etc. All these sources, including the background section, are used to construct the meaning of the claim terms. If any distinctions are made between the prior art and the present invention in the Background Section, these distinctions can, and will, be used to narrow the scope of patent protection.

24   *Leo Pharmaceutical Products LTD v. PTO* (Fed. Cir. August 12, 2013).

25   A third-party requests an *inter partes* reexamination at the USPTO to have a patent reexamined based on new prior art references (i.e., patents and printed publications of patent applications) to invalidate a patent or have the claims narrowed to avoid patent infringement liability.

26   During examination, the claimed invention was rejected and the inventors appealed the case to the Board of Patent Appeals and Interferences. During the appeal, the inventor showed that the prior art either discouraged combining vitamin D and corticosteroids in a single formulation or had attempted the combination without recognizing or solving the storage stability problems associated with combining the two. They showed that the prior art taught away from solving the store stability problems and they won the appeal. Here is a relevant quote from the case: "The inventors of the '013 patent *recognized* and solved a problem with the storage stability of certain formulations – a problem that the prior art *did not recognize* and a problem that was not solved for over a decade. As an initial matter, an invention can often be the recognition of the problem itself" (emphasis mine).

27   *Ultimate Pointer LLC v. Nintendo Co. Ltd.* (Fed. Cir. March 1, 2016).

28   The inventor drafted the patent to use the invention for conducting presentations. However, the inventor shifted the focus of the invention's use to games. This created significant problems in trying to broaden the patent beyond its originally designed purpose. Nevertheless, this case demonstrates that if the patent application disparages prior art, it may narrow the patent claims. Furthermore, if prior art problems need to be explained to secure a patent claim allowance, it may be preferable to explain the problems through the IDS or a telephonic interview where less written documentation (i.e., less evidence) is required as discussed in this chapter.

29   See Written description requirement in Section 2 for definition of antecedent basis.

30   This section discusses "literal infringement" only. It does not cover infringement under the Doctrine of Equivalents (DOE). To determine the proper scope of patent protection under an issued patent, including infringement under the DOE, an inventor will need to retain competent patent counsel, as DOE and claim interpretation is complex and ever-changing and therefore difficult to do without keeping up with the current state of the law.

31   By high value, I am referring to claims that can be used to stop entities from engaging in infringing actions. For example, a claim in which the end user is infringing on the patent may be generally less valuable than one in which a manufacturer would be infringing because suing all the end users would be unfeasible. It would be much simpler to enjoin the manufacturer to stop the infringing actions to prevent the end users' access to the infringing products.

32   One distinction between the role of the accused infringer and the examiner is that an accused infringer is an adversary to the patent owner whereas, the interaction between the examiner and the inventor is not an adversarial relationship. The examiner and inventor should cooperatively investigate the invention so that the inventor receives a patent only for inventions to which he or she is entitled under U.S. patent laws.

33   This does not necessarily mean that a claim to a method is useless. The end user's infringement liability can be attached to the manufacturer. A competitor can infringe on a product directly or indirectly. The manufacturer can infringe directly on the method of manufacturing claim but not the method of use claim. The manufacturer would be liable for the method of use claim according to the theory of indirect patent infringement. In this case, the manufacturer contributes to, or induces, the end user's direct infringement on the method of use claim. Therefore, the method of use claim provides valuable protection under a theory of indirect infringement. However, the method of manufacture claim would be more valuable for imposing patent infringement liability directly on the manufacturer.

34   See Appendix B for an example of how claims are numbered within the Claims Set.

35   Sometimes it is difficult to secure a patent on the method of manufacturing or even on the apparatus itself. In this case, securing a patent on the method of using the product from the perspective of the end user would enable a patent owner to sue, not the end user on the grounds of direct infringement, but the distributor on the grounds of indirect infringement. Direct infringement happens when an entity is personally engaging in the prohibited acts of making, using, selling, or offering to sell the patented product for use in the U.S., or importing the patented product into the U.S. Indirect infringement occurs when an entity is not directly infringing on the claims of the patent, but rather is contributing to someone else's direct infringement. Since the distributor is not *directly* infringing on the patent claim, the distributor may be sued according to the "theory of indirect infringement" for contributing to, or inducing, the end user's infringement. Claims that target a direct infringer are preferable because *indirect* infringement liability is more difficult to prove. It must be shown that the targeted entity is contributing to the direct infringement of another.

36   The first, parent patent is often the most valuable in an inventor's patent portfolio because it allows the inventor to mark the invention as patented with patent number. The product is no longer merely patent pending, but officially patented. This is called "patent marking" and it allows the inventor to place the public on notice of its patent. Patent marking places competitors that they can be held liable for damages for patent infringement beginning from either the time of infringement or patent marking, whichever occurs later. Patent marking acts as a constructive notice to competitors of the patent. Actual notice of the patent occurs when a patent owner sends a cease-and-desist letter to the accused infringer identifying the patent and infringing product. The first, parent patent also incurs additional costs to competitors because they must hire their own patent attorneys to determine the scope of patent protection afforded under the first patent.

37   Drawings cannot include shades and should be presented in solid black lines. Textual information should be minimal and no smaller than one eighth of an inch.

38   I utilize the services of www.patentsink.com and www.globalpatentgraphics.com

39   Bimeda R & D *Limited* (Fed. Cir. July 25, 2013).

40   Normally, each word is defined according to its ordinary, dictionary meaning unless the inventor acts as his or her own lexicographer. However, to alter the common meaning of a word, the inventor must clearly express that intent in the patent specification or prosecution history.

41   *Cadence Pharmaceutical v. Exela Pharm Sci Inc.* (Fed. Cir. 2015).

42   *Verderi, LLC v. Google, Inc.* (Fed. Cir. March 14, 2014).

43   Elevation refers to a type of view, such as top view, side view, bottom view, etc. An elevation view generally refers to a two-dimensional drawing of the front and sides of a building used in architectural drawings.

44   Meaning the scope of the claims does not include curved or spherical depictions. If the phrase "substantially elevations" excludes curved or spherical depictions and an accused infringing device includes curved or spherical depictions, the latter does not infringe on the claim. Conversely, if the phrase "substantially elevations" can include curved or spherical depictions and if an accused infringing device includes curved or spherical depictions, the latter infringes on the claim.

45   *Pacing Technologies, LLC. v. Garmin International, Inc.* (Fed. Cir. 2015).

46   *Kennametal, Inc. v. Ingersoll Cutting Tool Co.*, 780 F.3d 1376, (Fed. Cir. March 25, 2015).

47   Ingersoll (Defendant) petitioned the USPTO to reexamine Kennametal's patent in light of the Grab prior art patent reference, which expressly disclosed all of the limitations of Kennametal's claimed invention except for the method of applying the ruthenium binder via PVD process. The prior art reference mentioned ruthenium being applied with the PVD method but only as a side note ("However, applicants also contemplate that one or more layers of a coating scheme may be applied by physical vapor deposition (PVD).") Kennametal argued that Grab did not disclose the PVD method. The examples in the Grab reference only focused on two other unrelated, preferred methods of ruthenium application, mentioning PVD only as a "contemplated" method. Kennametal argued that, according to the Grab reference, one could not "immediately envisage" ruthenium being applied by PVD and it could not therefore be characterized as disclosing such information in order to invalidate Kennametal's patent. The Grab reference disclosed many different base materials and combinations thereof as well as three different methods of applying those materials. According to Kennametal, a total of 10,881 different combinations of binder materials and processes for applying them existed within the disclosure of the Grab reference. Kennametal asserted that the large number of possibilities negated the disclosure of any one specific combination except those "immediately envisaged" according to the description of the Grab reference. The specific examples highlighted in the specification are immediately envisaged and disclosed in the specification. But what about the other combinations? The Federal Circuit reasoned that since Claim 5 of the Grab reference recited five different

materials (including ruthenium), and the patent disclosed only three different coating methods (including PVD), the Grab patent disclosed only fifteen, not 10,881 combinations. Grab's explicit "contemplation" of PVD was sufficient evidence that a reader would immediately envisage applying ruthenium as a binder using PVD.

48   *Ineos USA LLC v. Berry Plastic Corp.* (Fed. Cir. 2015).

49   The algorithm should be expressed in "any understandable terms including a mathematical formula, in prose or as a flowchart, or in any other manner that provide sufficient structure."

50   *Augme Technologies v. Yahoo* (Fed. Cir. 2014). In this case, the court invalidated Claims 19 and 20 of United States Patent No. 6,594,691 for being indefinite. Claims 19 and 20 recited a means for assembling said second server, said second computer readable code module. The patent owner contended that the specification disclosed an algorithm for assembling the second computer readable code module in Figure 5 and column 11, line 60–column 12, line 1 and column 4, lines 51–60 of United States Patent No. 6,594,691. Shown below are the actual figures and verbiage recited by the patent owner in support of definiteness.

51   As previously mentioned, provisional applications are never examined. For more on the difference between provisional and nonprovisional applications, see Chapter 9.

52   See Chapter 7, step #3 for more information about filing for expedited examination.

53   The fee varies and depends on the entity size of the entity (i.e., patent applicant). A large entity will pay the standard rate, a small entity (~500 employees) about fifty percent of the standard rate, and a micro entity about twenty-five percent of the standard rate. Appendix E explains the differences between large, small, and micro entities and shows government filing fees for those entities.

54   In my experience, patents with petition to "make special based on age" often fall through the cracks. This is because, unlike for Track One requests, the USTPO does not have a tickle report (i.e., a reminder) that tells the supervisory patent examiner to place a patent application with a granted petition to make special on docket.

55   37 C.F.R. §1.56, 1.97-98.

56   See Chapter 7 for more information on Information Disclosure Statements.

57   The nonpublication request was created when the United States began publishing all patent applications eighteen months after the earliest priority date, that is, the filing date of the first filed application to which the instant application claims priority. For example, if a provisional application is filed and a subsequent nonprovisional application is filed one year later, the scheduled publication of the nonprovisional patent application will be eighteen months from the filing date

of the provisional application or six months after the filing of the nonprovisional application. The purpose was to move towards uniformity with patent laws of foreign countries and accordance with the American Inventors Protection Act. Most foreign, patent offices require that patent applications be published eighteen months after filing without an option to request nonpublication. Since the eighteen-month, pre-grant publication regime was an effort to harmonize U.S. patent laws with the patent laws in foreign countries, the United States created the non-publication request as a way for applicants who do not want to file in foreign countries to opt out of the eighteen-month, pre-grant publication requirement.

58   See Chapter 6 for more information on filing a patent application in foreign countries.

59   Annuities are payments made to foreign patent offices to maintain a patent application's pendency. By contrast, the USPTO does not collect annuities.

60   For more information on continuing applications, see the FAQ #22-29 below.

61   See 35 U.S.C. § 120 in Appendix F.

62   Most patents from related patent applications expire on the same date unless there are patent term adjustments that account for delays made by the USPTO, which are generally ninety to 180 days but may be significantly longer. Citation: http://patentlyo.com/patent/2016/11/patent- adjustment-statistics.html

63   See 35 U.S.C. § 102 and 35 U.S.C § 103 respectively in Appendix F.

64   See Chapter 10 for information on other substantive requirements such as the Written Description and Enablement requirements.

65   35 U.S.C. § 103 (See Appendix F).

66   Another way for protecting cornerstone technology is to approach the patent application process with a kitchen sink mentality. This means that the patent application will include everything about the cornerstone technology and all other bells and whistles and features peripheral to the cornerstone technology. The idea is that this omnibus patent application, over the course of many continuing applications, would have claims directed to different parts of the cornerstone technology, its peripheral features, and its benefits that would be submitted for examination in order to build a patent portfolio that protects both the cornerstone technology and its peripheral features.

67   See Appendix F.

68   Although a trademark technically refers to products while a service mark refers to services, I use the term "trademark" to refer to both because the tests for protection and enforcement are basically the same. A tradename is different from a trademark or service mark. A trademark is a brand associated with the product or service that comes to the mind of the consumer and a tradename is merely a company name.

About the Author

James Yang's well-rounded professional background allows him to offer a unique and valuable experience to his clients. He serves start-ups and midsize businesses, aiming to offer cost-effective legal advice and develop valuable patent protection that fits with their vision and values. He focuses his practice on all aspects of developing patent portfolios and prosecuting patent applications before the United States Patent and Trademark Office.

James earned his Bachelor of Science degree in mechanical engineering from California State Polytechnic University in Pomona, a school recognized for its engineering program. Before entering the legal field, he worked extensively in different areas of mechanical engineering. For several years, he managed a folding carton business where he acquired hands-on experience with automated machinery, printing equipment, die-cutting machines, and all aspects of paper-box manufacturing. This experience helps him to understand the challenges that inventors go through to launch their own product. He also worked as a mechanical engineer for Avibank Manufacturing, a supplier of custom fasteners for the aerospace industry, where he designed products for companies such as Boeing. Shortly before entering law school, he worked as a project manager at ACL Technologies installing multi-million-dollar pneumatic test facilities for the Taiwan Air Force.

James obtained his Juris Doctorate degree from Loyola Law School in Los Angeles. While attending law school, he was employed as a law clerk with a prominent Orange County law firm. This allowed him to utilize his legal studies in a real-world environment and practice under the guidance of seasoned attorneys. After his graduation from Loyola Law School in 2003, he accepted a position with this law firm as a patent attorney.

Working with a variety of clients, James has extensive experience in all areas of intellectual property law, patent strategy, and patent prosecution. His technology focus includes all types of simple to complex mechanical inventions, and his background in mechanical engineering greatly enhances his technical understanding of the intricacies of mechanical inventions.

James' accolades include Rising Star by Super Lawyers, 10.0 Avvo Rating, AV Preeminent.

* * *

Alateen hope for children of alcoholics

Al-Anon Family Group

DATE DUE	BORROWER'S NAME	ROOM NO.
	UPI 210-3301 Printed in USA	

DATE DUE	BORROWER'S NAME	ROOM NO.